VANISHED
TRUE STORIES
OF THE MISSING .

VANISHED
TRUE STORIES
OF THE MISSING

MARC TYLER NOBLEMAN

SCHOLASTIC INC.

New York   Toronto   London   Auckland
Sydney   Mexico City   New Delhi   Hong Kong

ISBN: 978-0-545-14472-8

12 11 10 9 8 7 6 5 4 3 2 1   10 11 12 13 14 15/0

Printed in the U.S.A.
First Scholastic printing, January 2010
Book design by Jennifer Rinaldi Windau

TO CHRISTIAN,
WHO KNOWS TOO MUCH ABOUT MISSING SOMEONE
AND WHO HAS NOT VANISHED AFTER ALL THESE YEARS.

CONTENTS

INTRODUCTION
SOMEWHERE OUT THERE

Everyday life throws at us a series of minor disappearing acts—the TV remote, the last cookie, the other sock.

This book is about life's *serious* disappearing acts—when a *person* vanishes, sometimes for good.

The stories you're about to read take you from the streets of Philadelphia to the jungles of Brazil. They go back in time, from 1925 to 2009. They introduce you to people ages five to fifty-eight. And each story is true.

You will puzzle over the fate of the author of one of the world's most popular children's books. You will meet a jazzman who staged one of the most startling comebacks in music history. You may stand up and pump your fist when you learn how a brave girl handled one of the scariest situations imaginable.

You also may notice that a certain missing person is, well, missing from this book. I did not feature one of the most famous vanishing acts in modern history—Amelia Earhart. Her story has been told often and well. I wanted to tell stories you may *not* know the endings to already.

When someone disappears, his or her loved ones are devastated. That fear of the unknown can eat away at a person. But even though this book includes stories of people who were never seen again, it is balanced with tales of people who *did* return, often against astounding odds and always under surprising circumstances.

Many disappearances lead to despair for those left behind. Yet at the same time, many lead to hope. Many bring out strength in people that they didn't know they had—both the people waiting for good news and the people out there somewhere, wanting nothing more than to be found.

ESCAPE FROM THE BASEMENT
SECOND-GRADER ERICA PRATT

Seven-year-old Erica Pratt was growing up happy in a hard place. Her Southwest Philadelphia neighborhood was poor and plagued by crime—from robbery to murder. Some houses in the area were beautifully maintained with quiet pride, but too many were falling apart or boarded up.

Erica lived with her grandmother, Barbara Pratt, and her five-year-old sister, Naliyah. Barbara made sure the girls had a loving home no matter how dangerous it could be down the block. She didn't let the girls wander far on their own.

One summer evening, the sisters were walking home. They were nearly there when a car pulled up. In seconds, Erica became the victim of one type of crime that was rare in their crime-ridden neighborhood: She was kidnapped.

Her family was in shock. Every second that Erica was missing felt like an hour, and every hour felt like forever.

— — — —

1

Twenty-nine-year-old James Burns and twenty-three-year-old Edward Johnson both had long criminal records. Together, they were planning their next crime. To prepare, they had been secretly watching the Pratt family for two weeks.

With her warm brown eyes, wide smile, and braided ponytails, Erica practically shimmered with charm. Erica's family adored her. Her teachers did, too. And she had a rascally sense of humor. At a sleepover, she poured a bit of water on a friend's blanket to try to make her think she had wet the bed. It didn't take long for her friend and the other girls to realize that Erica (or "E," as she was sometimes called) had played a prank, and they laughed.

Erica's mother, Sarina, was young when Erica was born. Sarina didn't feel ready to be a mother. Erica's father, Eric, had gotten into trouble with the law and couldn't be a full-time parent, either. Sarina and Eric split up. Luckily for the family, Erica's grandmother had a helping heart and a stockpile of strength. She took in Erica and Naliyah to raise them. Sarina lived around the corner from her daughters.

Monday, July 22, 2002, started as a typical Philadelphia summer night—in terms of weather, anyway. Neighbors stood or sat on stoops and steps, gossiping in the sweltering heat. Erica and Naliyah headed home on the sidewalk. At 9:20 PM, a beat-up white car with tinted windows stopped next to the girls.

"Erica, come here," an unfamiliar voice said from the car.

A large man in a white T-shirt and baseball cap—Edward—darted out and grabbed Erica. She did not know him. In a panic, Erica grabbed Naliyah's hand—not to pull Naliyah with her, but hoping her little sister could somehow pull *her* away. Erica screamed and tried to kick free. No one seemed to hear or see her. It was happening so fast.

"Come on, let's get out of here!" the driver—James—said.

Edward picked up and carried thirty-pound, three-foot-five-inch-tall Erica into the car. To stop her from squirming, he held her between his knees. James sped off as Edward wrapped duct tape over her eyes.

Naliyah bolted toward home, sobbing and shouting, "A man took Erica! They took her from me!"

Neighbors ran to Naliyah and tried to calm her down so they could find out what happened. She didn't know the names of the men. She didn't know the license plate of the car. She knew only that, with the screech of tires, her sister was gone.

— — — —

Erica was not the only girl snatched by a stranger in the summer of 2002. Kidnappings in Utah and California also made the news. It seemed as though the country was experiencing a rise in child abductions. However, that was not true—it was an increase in the media coverage of abductions that made it feel that way. One child-abduction story is one too many, so multiple abduction stories upset the public unbearably.

Erica's case was different from the other high-profile abductions that summer. The other kidnapped girls were white and from well-off families. Erica was African-American and from a low-income family.

Though no one could know it at the time, Erica's story would soon turn out to be different in a *second* significant way.

According to the FBI, it is critical to rescue a kidnapped child within the first twenty-four hours after they have been abducted because, once that much time has elapsed, the child is at even greater risk of injury or death. The police began to hunt for Erica's kidnappers immediately. At the same time, Erica's neighbors began a hunt of their own. They walked up and down the streets calling her name. Some of them would keep at it until sunrise the next morning.

Edward and James took Erica to an empty house in North

Philadelphia, twelve miles away. The house had been abandoned for several years, although a few months earlier, someone had begun to renovate it before moving in. In the meantime, the house did have a *few* occupants—after the previous occupants had moved out, raccoons and possums had moved in.

The kidnappers took Erica down to the dark, damp basement. Paint was crumbling off the walls. Cinder blocks sat like stone stumps on the concrete floor. Old pipes snaked silently behind broken or unfinished walls.

Using more duct tape, the kidnappers bound Erica's hands and feet and put her on a filthy mattress. If Erica's eyes hadn't been taped over, she might have noticed the rose prints decorating the mattress; those faded flowers might have been her only reminder at that moment that there was still beauty in the world.

Twenty minutes after Erica was taken, a man called her grandmother and said the Pratt family would have to pay "a hundred and fifty" or else they would not see Erica again.

"A hundred and fifty dollars?" Barbara said.

"No," the man said. "A hundred and fifty thousand dollars."

"There's not a hundred and fifty thousand dollars in this whole neighborhood," a friend said to the family.

The caller, however, believed that the Pratt family *did* have the money, and he called back at least five more times that night. In a call just before midnight, the caller let Erica speak with her mother and grandmother. A police officer later explained that the kidnappers might have had Barbara's phone number simply because they made Erica give it to them—or maybe because they already knew the family. *Something* had convinced the men that the Pratts had $150,000.

The police assured the Pratt family that their priority was to return Erica safely to them as soon as possible. Sarina didn't sleep all night. Family members cried.

Edward and James told Erica that her family would have to give them money to get her back. They left her a bottle of juice and a bag of potato chips. Then they just left her alone.

Erica did not know where she was and when—or if—the men would return. She didn't know what time it was. She assumed that people were looking for her and took some comfort in that, but she wished they would hurry up. In the meantime, she realized she should not just sit and wait.

She had to try to do something to help herself.

She decided to use her winning smile as a weapon.

Sometime during the night, she began to gnaw at the duct tape around her hands.

Tuesday dawned on another hot day in Philadelphia. Two people who had witnessed Erica's abduction tipped off the police with the names of the abductors. The police were combing the neighborhood looking for Edward and James and, most urgently, Erica. Organizations and individuals who'd heard of Erica's abduction offered reward money for finding her. Within a day, the amount reached $10,000.

After hours of chewing on the thick gray tape, Erica broke all the way through. It had tasted foul, but she was free—partly. She unwrapped the tape from over her eyes and yanked off the tape around her feet.

Even though it was still light outside, she couldn't see in the windowless basement. She felt her way until she came to a door that opened to another part of the basement. She carefully made her way up a staircase that was full of holes. At the top of the stairs was another door—and it was locked.

Erica kicked a wooden panel of the door, and it popped out. After squeezing through the narrow hole it left, she made her way through the house, not knowing if the kidnappers would suddenly appear and stop her. She made it to the front door—which was also locked. But that door had no panel to try to kick out.

She went to a window and screamed for help.

Nearby, a five-foot-tall thirteen-year-old named Dustin Ballard was hanging out with a friend at a popular meeting spot for kids in the neighborhood, a big oak tree. None of them had heard that a girl had been kidnapped. Dustin was about to head to a convenience store when he heard someone calling from the abandoned house, "Help me!"

At first, Dustin thought it was a ghost. None of the kids nearby wanted to go near the house to check it out.

When the cries for help persisted, Dustin swallowed his fear. With seventeen-year-old Vanessa Ponds, he followed the voice. The two teens ran across the street to the two-story house where Erica was trapped. Weeds choked the front yard, which was enclosed by a metal fence. They saw movement through one of the tall windows next to the front door. Someone was banging on the window—not a ghost but a girl.

Dustin and Vanessa rushed up onto the front porch. From inside, Erica opened the mail slot in the door. Vanessa peeked through and saw eyes red from crying. Erica had found a set of keys in the house and pushed them through the slot. Vanessa tried to unlock the door with them, but none worked. She told Erica to break one of the windows.

Erica went back into the house and found a rubber mallet that was being used in the renovation. She swung it against a front window, which shattered. Dustin punched through the storm window and screen on his side of the window, then ripped it apart more, scratching up his hand in the process. He took away some of the broken glass so he and Vanessa could pull Erica through without cutting anyone. Dustin reached in, lifted Erica, and cradled her.

"Thank you, thank you," Erica said. She had pieces of duct tape and adhesive marks on her body and in her hair. She told Dustin and Vanessa where she lived. It was nearly eight PM—almost a day after Erica had been kidnapped. She was no longer missing, but her ordeal was not over yet.

— — — —

Vanessa hopped on her bike to get help. She found Michael Harvey and Andrew Skaziak, police officers on duty as part of a program called Operation Safe Streets. When Vanessa told them what just happened, the officers thought this might be the girl everyone was looking for. But they also thought it might not be Erica, because the house the girl had been in was fairly close to the scene of the crime. The officers expected kidnappers to take a ransom victim farther away than that.

They went to Erica. She was wearing a white tank top and blue shorts—which matched the description of the kidnapped girl. This was indeed Erica Pratt. The police, family, friends, neighbors, and even the FBI had all been searching for her ... and the hero who ended up saving her was herself. "Erica did the work," Officer Harvey said.

That was the second significant way Erica's abduction differed from others that summer.

Erica's eye was swollen, but she didn't seem to have any other physical health problems. The officers asked her questions and she answered clearly. She wasn't crying. She was hungry. They put her in their patrol car, and Officer Skaziak gave her a chicken sandwich he hadn't eaten.

Dustin and Vanessa had slipped away. The officers tried to find them, but the streets were crowded. "They are heroes as well," Officer Skaziak said.

Police surrounded and searched the house. The kidnappers

were not there, but once Edward's fingerprints were confirmed to be on the duct tape, the police could focus on apprehending him and James.

Erica was taken to the hospital. The cornea of the swollen eye had been scratched, probably by the duct tape. Otherwise she was fine.

As the medical staff removed the bits of duct tape from Erica's body, she broke down and cried. But when her grandmother walked in, the tears vanished. It was all kisses and hugs from then on.

Around eleven PM, Erica was released from the hospital. Television news crews were waiting in front of her home. As a kind female police officer carried her by, Erica waved to them. Neighbors cheered her return.

The next day, the family was showered with attention. People called from across the country to wish the family well and sent bouquets of balloons. Strangers wanted to send money to start a college fund for Erica.

A woman from South Carolina said that Erica was "destined to be a strong voice in our society. One day, she might stand up again, not to a kidnapper, but for all of us. I want her to know that there is good in this world and good people that care." A woman from Maryland said about Erica, "Usually when you have families that experience lots of pain, there's always going to be one that's going to make it. She was determined to live."

Meanwhile, Erica's eye was already better, and she went right back to doing what she loved: painting, making beaded necklaces, running around with friends, and eating ice-cream sandwiches.

The family appeared before the press. One of Erica's uncles held her while another acted as the family spokesperson. Erica's family hadn't let her watch news about herself. They didn't want to discuss with her what she had been through, and they didn't want anyone else to do that, either. "If she's forgotten about what happened, I'd just as soon it would stay forgotten," her uncle said. He asked that the reporters' questions focus on the family's happiness that Erica was back.

As her uncle spoke, Erica hid her face against the stuffed dog she held. At one point she dropped it. Her friend Shenay handed it back to her.

"We missed you," Shenay said. "I was crying."

"For real?" Erica asked, lifting her head off her uncle's shoulder. She chose not to say anything to the reporters.

Her uncle thanked the community for its support and said the

Pratts would send a special thank-you to the young people and police officers who helped rescue Erica. Her loved ones credited Erica's street smarts for the rest.

"I have twenty-one years in the police department," Philadelphia's police inspector, William Colarulo, said, "and I have never seen this kind of heroic act of bravery committed by a seven-year-old."

"Most children would have been afraid, would have sat there and cried," Erica's neighbor said. "Most adults, also."

A family friend said, "You don't mess with a seven-year-old from Southwest Philadelphia."

"Our biggest concern is that the baby come back to us in good health, and this is what she did," Erica's great-grandmother, Geraldine Tate, said.

That night, a local basketball league in which one of Erica's uncles coached called off their game out of respect for the family.

Before dawn Thursday morning, police officers saw Edward and James in a parked car not far from the Pratt home. The kidnappers knew the police were looking for them—Erica's story had been all over the news for four days. But they probably didn't know that the police knew they had been trying to get ahold of enough money to get out of the city. The police had traced their cell phone calls and had the Pratts' neighborhood under surveillance.

As the officers approached the kidnappers, Edward and James noticed them and scrambled from the car, each in a different direction. James's sneakers fell off as he ran. After a foot chase, the police caught up with both of them. James had climbed to the roof of a one-story garage and was lying on his back.

"It's over," the officer said, handcuffing him.

In custody, Edward said the two men kidnapped Erica because they had heard that the Pratt family had just been given $150,000 in life-insurance money for one of Erica's uncles who had been shot and killed earlier that year. However, it was a false rumor.

Edward and James did not target Erica specifically. They planned to take the first family member they spotted. After the kidnappers found out that the police knew they had taken Erica, they left her in the house, planning not to return. When James was caught, the key to the house was still in his pocket.

Though it was scary for her, Erica identified Edward as the man who had grabbed her. James apologized to the Pratt family. Both men were charged with multiple crimes and pleaded guilty. They were given long jail sentences.

A local organization honored Erica, Dustin, Vanessa, and several other children who had assisted them by giving them plaques for their bravery. *Time* magazine named Erica the Person of the Week. Black Entertainment Television (BET) named her the Person of the Year for 2002. In 2003, the Justice Department's National Center for Missing and Exploited Children awarded Erica the National Courage Award.

Erica's disappearance brought her neighborhood together in a way few would have predicted. Her return brought people even closer.

Nothing that starts off with a child in danger can have a completely happy ending—the child may never forget the fear she felt—but Erica's story comes close. She may have felt afraid, but she didn't feel helpless.

THE REAL INDIANA JONES
EXPLORER PERCY FAWCETT

Dangers fast, silent, and unseen lurk in Brazil's Amazon rain forests. Colonel Percy Fawcett faced most of them and was afraid of none of them, or so it seemed. He knew how to survive in the wild, but he had more than his share of luck, too.

Once, a jaguar tried to attack Percy, but the explorer managed to get away. Various native tribes lived in the jungle, and some were displeased when outsiders such as Percy intruded. More than once, Percy and his companions were the targets of six-foot-long poisoned arrows, but Percy never became a bull's-eye. When Percy and his mule accidentally tumbled into a churning stream, Percy climbed out onto the bank unhurt. He battled a huge spider that had crawled into his sleeping bag and then onto his hand, shaking it away before it could deliver its poisonous bite.

Between 1906 and 1924, the tall British explorer with a handlebar mustache made seven trips into the rain forests of South America. He was looking for adventure. Specifically, he was looking for a lost city that was supposedly hidden in the depths of the jungle. Percy didn't know if the lost city was real. But if it was, he was determined to find it.

In 1925, Percy, his twenty-year-old son, Jack, and Jack's friend Raleigh Rimell planned to head into a certain area of the rain forest. A native tribe they had been with urged them not to go there—it was home to fierce natives. Percy was sure he could handle it, just like he'd handled so much else.

Ignoring the tribe's warning, the three men pushed on into the dense green foliage. They never came out.

— — — —

Born in 1867, Percy did as his parents wanted and joined the Royal Artillery, a branch of the British army, at age nineteen. He married Nina Paterson and was transferred from Ceylon (now Sri Lanka) to North Africa, where he worked for the British secret service. Percy did not smoke or drink alcohol. While other soldiers relaxed, Percy explored the nearby ancient ruins by himself.

Percy wanted a different type of adventure from what the military offered. He studied to become a surveyor, a person who measures land to set boundaries or make maps. In early 1906, the president of the Royal Geographical Society (RGS)—Percy's father had been a member—showed Percy a chart of South America. "It's full of blank spaces because so little is known of it," he said. A better map was needed.

The RGS president went on to explain that both Bolivia and Brazil wanted control of the rubber-tree forests between their nations. The worldwide demand for rubber was high, which meant that any country selling rubber could make a good profit. If a clearly defined border couldn't be established, the two countries might go to war.

Bolivia and Brazil agreed that the fairest way to survey their mutual border was to get a trustworthy third party to do it. They asked the RGS, and the RGS asked Percy. He said yes immediately. Though Percy was unfamiliar with the dangers and challenges of the region, he did know that such a job would also be an adventure. It was a time when foreign travel was a luxury few people could afford or were interested in.

After arriving in Bolivia in June, Percy learned that the journey to the area he had to survey would be tougher than he had anticipated.

The trail to the survey area wound high into the mountains. It was so steep that Percy's pack mules could not climb more than thirty feet without stopping and gasping for breath. Percy feared the trek might be so exhausting for the mules that they would not survive it.

Water travel was also treacherous. Once, Percy and several others were on wooden rafts when the river current picked up significantly. They were sent hurtling down the river far too fast for comfort, but then the river widened and they slowed down. Relieved that the worst was over, they drifted around a large rock formation and realized they may have been mistaken. They heard a loud sound up ahead—a waterfall.

One of the rafts in the party managed to get to the riverbank, but Percy's didn't. The current tossed the raft over the edge of the twenty-foot-high waterfall. The men were thrown from the raft, but all survived. However, they lost a good deal of their gear.

During another expedition, Percy and his party left the river and prepared to continue on foot. To make the journey easier, they buried some of their possessions in metal cases near where they had come ashore. Later, their food supply began to run low, and they had reached an area of the river where it was harder to find fish. They also struggled to catch any land animals to eat. One of Percy's native assistants wanted to give up. He lay down and told them to go on without him. Percy refused to leave him and gently poked him in the ribs to get him up.

For more than ten days, they lived on a few bird eggs and some spoiled honey. After the twentieth day, they were close to starvation. Finally they saw a deer, but it seemed out of gun range. Percy tried anyway—and despite his weakness, he killed the deer on the first shot. He and his party ate every possible part of that deer.

Various diseases such as influenza commonly spread among local people. Percy encountered one village where disease had killed half the population. Some of the diseases had been brought in by earlier European explorers.

Percy witnessed how Europeans and natives could be brutal to one another. Natives felt that Europeans were invading their territory. Europeans believed that natives were less civilized than they were. After a native killed a white man, the white man's brother took revenge by poisoning *eighty* natives.

Though slavery was illegal, Europeans would force entire native villages to work on their rubber plantations. Understandably, some natives began to react angrily at merely the sight of any white man. Percy was horrified that many of his fellow Europeans didn't care about the natives' human rights.

Percy's approach was different. He greeted and treated natives with kindness. When he passed through their territory, he gave them gifts. He patiently listened to their stories and was interested in their knowledge. He was fascinated that natives used their sense of smell to hunt, as animals do, and how they could make strange vocal sounds that attracted certain prey. He was intrigued that they knew of a plant whose juices could eat through metal and a sap that stunned but didn't poison fish.

Though Percy sincerely respected the natives, he understood why some of them might still distrust him. And some tribes had a hostile reputation no matter how peaceful visitors might be. Once, the boat Percy was on landed on the riverbank, and the pilot went alone to check out a nearby road. He didn't come back when expected, so Percy went to investigate and found the pilot dead. His body was pierced with forty-two arrows.

Wildlife was a constant threat. Jaguars prowled the jungle. Some spiders were big enough to catch and eat birds. Menacing-looking crocodiles stood guard along riverbanks. Ants that bit and blood-sucking cockroaches swarmed the ground and greenery. At night, vampire bats swooped down to drink blood. The mosquitoes were overwhelming. The men slept under mosquito nets, but if any part of their bodies poked out, it would become riddled with bites.

In his travels, Percy had to cross multiple rivers. Sometimes he swam across to attach a rope to the other side so his party could pull across their equipment. South American rivers were often thick with piranha fish. Piranhas have a reputation for being man-eaters. While that is not fully accurate, piranhas may attack a person who has a wound or even a small cut. When a member of Percy's party rinsed blood from his hands in a river, piranhas bit off two of his fingers.

Wild bulls posed a problem on more than one occasion. One day, three bulls charged Percy and his group as they rode in an oxcart. The men drove off the bulls with gunshots. Another day, a bull positioned itself between Percy, who was on foot, and the cart ahead of him. Percy wasn't carrying a gun. No trees or other escape options were nearby. Percy looked purposefully at the snorting beast and slowly walked around it. Somehow his stare saved his life.

If anything rattled Percy, it was snakes. Once, a seven-foot-long poisonous snake lunged at one of Percy's companions. The companion managed to shoot and kill the snake, but then he noticed he had been bitten—rather, his tobacco pouch had been.

If not for that pouch, the snake's venomous fangs would have punctured the man's skin and likely killed him.

The Amazon was home to many kinds of snakes, including some that wailed. Other snake species were said to be enormous. The natives insisted that giant anacondas were real. Percy's hunger for excitement was stronger than his aversion to snakes. He wanted to not only see but also capture a giant anaconda. In 1907, he got his chance.

Traveling with his party on a slow-moving river, Percy noticed movement underneath their boat. He made out a triangular shape attached to a long, curvy stem. Percy probably knew what it was before the giant anaconda broke the surface of the water. He barely had time to aim his rifle, but successfully hit the snake in the spine. Sizing up the body onshore, Percy guessed it was sixty-two feet long—far longer than any snake on record. When word spread to the scientific community, most thought Percy was mistaken—or lying.

Even wildlife not visible to the naked eye was harmful. If a certain kind of tapeworm got into a person's digestive system, it had the strange effect of causing the person to want to eat dirt.

Despite the many daily risks during the survey, Percy did not get sick or seriously injured even once. The survey took three years, but once it was finished in 1909, Percy knew he would someday return to South America. There was so much more to explore.

— — — —

Percy had made his first trip to the South American jungle to do work for someone else. Each time he returned, it was for himself. After his survey, Percy retired from the military. From then on, he raised funds from private sources to pay for his expeditions. Percy had difficulty finding people to go with him—the trips were long and dangerous. Yet he always managed.

During a 1910 expedition, as Percy and his party paddled up a river, they startled a native tribe on a sandbar. "Dogs barked, men shouted, women screamed and reached for their children," Percy said. Then the arrows began to fly.

As his party members ducked, Percy tried to calm the natives by saying what he could in their language. However, the natives continued to shoot arrows at them. Percy was willing to try most anything, so he told one of the men in the boat to play his accordion. After several peppy songs, the Indians stopped the attack—and then even welcomed Percy. Yet again, Percy's diplomacy earned him friends.

In 1912, the first book about Percy's South American adventures was published—sort of. The bestselling book was titled *The Lost World* and it was written by Sir Arthur Conan Doyle, who also created the famous detective Sherlock Holmes. *The Lost World* was fictional, but it was inspired by Percy, a personal friend of the author's. The novel told of a professor who explores South America and discovers living prehistoric animals, including dinosaurs.

One night in 1913, Percy noticed eyes gleaming at him from just beyond the campfire light. It appeared to be a dog except for one quality—it had two noses. At first, the explorers thought that it must be a mutant dog. A local told them that other dogs like it lived in the area.

The name of the breed, Percy learned, is the double-nosed Andean tiger hound. Hunting in a pack, these dogs were able to take down a jaguar. (Locally, jaguars were called tigers, which is where the dog's name comes from.) Just like with the giant anaconda, many Europeans back home did not believe what Percy had seen was truly a double-nosed dog.

Percy claimed that he had come across other jungle animals that had not yet been documented by Europeans. Perhaps the most astonishing creature in that category was something resembling a diplodocus—a large dinosaur with an appetite for plants. Numerous Indian tribes claimed that such a reptile did indeed lumber through the dense jungle. Some explorers who did not encounter such an animal did see large tracks that seemed to fit the description. Perhaps *The Lost World* was not *entirely* fictional after all.

World War I broke out and Percy returned to England to serve his country. Shortly after the war ended, he was back in Brazil looking through old documents at a library in Rio de Janeiro. He read about a Portuguese man's quest in 1753 to find an ancient stone city of secrets in a valley between mountains in the Mato Grosso region of the Brazilian jungle. Various natives had told Percy legends of such a place as well. Some versions said this jungle city had a connection to the fabled lost city of Atlantis. One version said the buildings were filled with a mysterious light that scared those who saw it. However, neither the 1753 expedition nor any since had found any such city in the jungle.

Percy had already found animals in the jungle that others did not believe were real. He was confident that he could prove that this unknown city was real, too.

He named it "Z."

— — — —

In January 1925, Percy sailed from London to New York to Rio. From there, he took a train and then a steamboat deep into the wilderness. He wrote Nina that after entering the jungle, "we shall disappear from civilization until the end of next year." On April 20, he set off in search of the lost city of Z. On his previous expedition, he had found the remains of what he believed was a small settlement of people from Z, but he wanted to find the actual city.

He liked smaller-size expeditions. They were easier to manage and less intimidating to the natives. Therefore, this time, he had only two companions—his twenty-year-old son, Jack and Jack's friend and classmate Raleigh Rimell. Before leaving, Percy had requested that no rescue team look for them if they did not return, because it would be too dangerous.

As the trio tramped through fifteen hundred miles of jungle, Percy sent letters home to Brian, the younger of his two sons. Brian was thrilled to read about the distant adventures of his father and brother. Percy was familiar with only some of the territory they were moving through, but the map he used was incomplete. At one point, a tick bit Raleigh, and his foot became infected. He began to limp.

They reached the end of the area that Percy knew. Up until that point, Percy was almost always able to find a hut they could sleep in at night. Looking forward, all was a mystery. Percy sent back their native guides, preferring to move forward with only Jack and Raleigh, and on foot rather than by water. He gave the last returning guide a note to mail to Nina in which he wrote, "You need have no fear of any failure." On May 29, Percy sent what would be his last telegraph to her. He was excited to be so close to going from A(mazon) to Z.

It's a good thing that Percy was not the type of person who believed in bad omens. His last known rest stop was named Dead Horse Camp. His last known movement was a crossing of the Upper Xingu, a tributary of the Amazon River. That area was just beyond a body of water that natives called the River of Death.

Sometime after that crossing, Percy, Jack, and Raleigh vanished. No one back home heard from any of them ever again.

— — — —

Yet again, people did not heed Percy.

Because Percy said that he wouldn't return sooner than 1927, his loved ones were not deeply worried when they didn't hear from him for a while. But when Percy had still not emerged from the jungle by 1928, against Percy's wishes, a search party set out. George Dyott, who had met Percy only once, led the search.

Soon George understood how easily a person could disappear in Brazil. "We are surrounded by Indians at this place," he radioed, panic in his voice. George found a piece of Percy's map case in one village, but it didn't help answer the question of Percy's fate.

Members of the Kalapalo tribe told George of Percy's arrival at their village. He and his companions had walked in, the first Europeans many Kalapalos had seen. Percy had told the Kalapalos what he was trying to do, and they warned him not to go in the direction he planned, because fierce natives lived that way. Percy went anyway.

The Kalapalos saw smoke from Percy's campfires rising from the jungle each of the next four days. On the fifth day, there was no smoke. The Kalapalos took that as a sign that Percy and his two young companions had been killed. They accused a neighboring tribe.

Though he found no proof, George stated that, in July 1925, natives had clubbed all three men to death.

That conclusion did not satisfy everyone. George's search party was only the first—at least twelve more tried to learn for certain what happened to Percy. All told, more than one hundred people would lose their lives in search of the explorer. Nina held on to the hope that she would see her husband again, but sadly, she died without that happening.

Over the years, a few clues surfaced and many rumors swirled about Percy. In 1927, a navy officer noticed that a piece of a native's jewelry was the nameplate from one of Percy's carrying cases. In 1933, someone discovered a compass that had belonged to Percy near a tribe's camp. However, neither item led to Percy.

Some people thought he died of natural causes. Others assumed that natives or jaguars or some other jungle peril had killed him. Some rumors claimed that he had been captured and worshiped by natives and that he had many children in the jungle, the oldest of whom carried a golden spear. Natives reported seeing Percy in the jungle throughout the 1930s. There were rumors that he had become the head of a tribe of cannibals or that he had started his own cult. According to another rumor, Percy never planned to return to England and *did* find Z—where he was happy to stay.

In 1951, a man named Orlando Villas Boas claimed he had learned the truth about Percy's death. Orlando was a native who worked for the Brazilian government. He was known for standing up for the rights of native peoples. He had visited native villages in the Mato Grosso to ask if anyone had seen Percy.

According to Orlando, the chief of the Kalapalos confessed that his tribe had killed Percy because he had insulted them twice—by not sharing a duck he had killed and by slapping a Kalapalo child. Orlando said the Kalapalos dug up Percy's skeleton, which he would have scientifically examined. Orlando also said the tribe asked him to promise that no European planes would come to seek revenge if they told him how they killed Percy. Orlando assured them that Europeans did not plan to hurt them.

Percy's son Brian didn't believe what Orlando said. The skeleton was too short to be his father's. In time, the truth about Orlando's story came out. The Kalapalos said that Orlando had asked them to dig up the tallest skeleton they knew of so he could *pretend* it was Percy's. Apparently Orlando also made up the stories about the duck and the slapping. He may have done all that to scare off explorers and protect the natives. But to the Kalapalos, it seemed that their onetime friend Orlando, the great native defender, had betrayed them. He made them appear to be murderers. They insisted that they hadn't killed Percy.

Brian went twice to Brazil to search himself. He wrote a

note in the native languages of the local people asking for help in locating his father and brother and dropped copies of it over the region from an airplane. No one responded. In the jungle, Brian came across large limestone structures. Rain and wind had shaped them in such a way that Brian saw how a person could think they looked like an ancient city.

In 1953, Brian published *Lost Trails, Lost Cities* (also called *Exploration Fawcett*), a book of his father's letters and other writings. It was instantly popular. *Ruins in the Sky*, another book he wrote about his father, came out in 1957. Several other people, including George Dyott, also wrote books on Percy. Brian died in 1984, still not knowing what had happened to his father and brother.

In 1996, the Kalapalos seized twelve members of a sixteen-person expedition that had come in search of information on Percy. The Kalapalos still denied having anything to do with Percy's death. However, they took hostages to trade them for thirty thousand dollars' worth of equipment, including boats. All twelve explorers were released unharmed.

In search of a fabled lost city, Percy may well have gotten lost himself. Future expeditions may continue to scour the Brazilian jungle for any hint about what happened to him. By many accounts, Percy was a good man, but he did not actually do anything *historic*. What he is most famous for today is his disappearance.

He did earn another claim to fame, however, but many years after he vanished. Though the creators of the 1981 film *Raiders of the Lost Ark* have not publicly stated this, some people believe that Percy was an inspiration for the character Indiana Jones, the brilliant professor who has adventures around the world, can hold his own in tough situations—and dislikes snakes.

THE GOLDEN TREE KILLER
WOODSMAN GRANT HADWIN

Thomas Grant Hadwin disappeared a lot.

As a woodsman, disappearing was practically part of his job description. He had held multiple positions over the years, all involving the outdoors. He went by his middle name, Grant, and he often ventured alone into the deep forests of British Columbia, the westernmost province of Canada, for work.

On January 20, 1997, Grant again went into the forest, but this time not for work. Under cover of night, he did something extreme that upset many people. A few weeks later, he took off in a kayak and disappeared for good.

This time, as far as anyone knows, he never came back.

— — — —

Around 1700, a tree with a special destiny took root on Graham Island, the largest island of the Queen Charlotte Islands, sixty miles off the coast of British Columbia and thirty miles south of Alaska. Approximately five thousand people live there, two thousand of whom are members of the Haida tribe. These native people call the islands Haida Gwaii ("Land of the Haida"). Generations of Haida have considered this tree sacred. In the twentieth century, almost anyone who went to the Queen Charlottes heard of this tree.

The Queen Charlotte Islands comprise two main islands and at least one hundred and fifty smaller ones. The landscape of many of these islands looks the same as it would have hundreds of years ago. Mist commonly hovers over the islands, blocking sunlight. Old-growth temperate rain forests grow right up to the sea. When ocean waves swell, they can pound into the woods, sometimes hurling fish into branches.

Tree trunks are monstrous and packed together tightly. The top of the forest is a dense green canopy of leaves and clumps of moss, preventing any sunlight that may pierce the mist from reaching the toadstools and gnarled roots on the forest floor. One Haida said the Queen Charlottes look like the planet of Yoda, the wrinkled, green-skinned Jedi who mentored young Luke Skywalker in the *Star Wars* movies.

Adding to this moody atmosphere is a distinctly human contribution—totem poles. These towering wooden carvings stand guard along beaches, unmoved since they were put there—in some cases more than a century ago.

Bald eagles soar overhead, as if they are the region's guardians. Bears can grow as big as cars. Sea otters once frolicked plentifully offshore until hunters killed them off to sell their pelts, but whales still call these waters home. In 1996, people discovered an albino raven living in the Queen Charlottes. Tourists flocked to see the bird until it was accidentally killed the next year.

As popular as the white raven was, the superstar attraction of the Queen Charlottes was a three-hundred-year-old tree, a Sitka spruce. It began as a seed shaped like a teardrop and grew on the bank of the Yakoun River—one hundred and sixty feet tall, the equivalent of sixteen stories. Its trunk was more than six feet in diameter. Those qualities, however, did not distinguish it—many trees in the region were as big, or bigger.

Like the albino raven, this spruce was an unusual color—and shape—for its species. Sitka spruces typically have green needles and a furry, uneven appearance. This tree had golden needles and a smooth cone shape. Separately, these would have been eye-catching features, but together, they made this tree a breathtaking sight. Some said it looked as if it glowed from inside. To people flying over the forest, it stood out like a lone candle flickering during a blackout.

One visitor nicknamed the golden spruce the "Ooh-Aah Tree" because that was what she said when she first saw it. Decades earlier, the Haida had given it a name, too—K'iid K'iyass, which means "Elder Spruce Tree."

Though rare, other golden spruces supposedly existed in the area and possibly elsewhere. But none known was as golden, as big, or as neatly formed as K'iid K'iyass. It seemed unique and held great spiritual value to the Haida.

The native people told different stories to explain how the mutant tree came to be. One describes an ancient village whose residents did not treat one another well. To punish them, the Creator sent a snowstorm that smothered the village until all the people were dead, except two—a boy and his grandfather.

Despite the blizzard, these two managed to flee the village. The grandfather warned the boy not to look back, but the boy did not listen. He turned around toward his ruined home, so the Creator transformed him into a tree—a golden spruce. The Haida say that their tribe will admire the golden spruce until their last generation.

Non-Haida also searched for an explanation for the tree. The first recorded foreigner to see the golden spruce was a Scottish timber surveyor, in 1924. He was shocked and later said he didn't cut it down because it was seemingly one of a kind. Other observers wondered if the tree was yellow because it had been struck by lightning or because it was an undocumented species.

Scientists sought a botanical explanation for the golden needles. When one perplexed forestry expert was asked what could cause such a phenomenon, her answer was, "Magic!" Plants need sunlight to survive. They use light to produce their own food in a process called photosynthesis. The chemical inside plants that allows them to do this—and that makes most of them green—is called chlorophyll.

Some scientists theorize that, with the golden spruce, sunlight may have had the opposite effect—a harmful one. Perhaps sunlight somehow changed the chlorophyll, turning normally green needles to yellow. While sunlight usually helps plants live, it could have been killing the golden spruce, except for one fact—the golden spruce was very much alive.

Maybe the forestry expert was right. Maybe the tree was magical after all.

- - - -

More than 250 years after the sapling that would become the golden spruce poked from the ground, Grant Hadwin entered the world.

Grant was born in West Vancouver, British Columbia, and lived there with his parents and brother (who was twelve years older). He played tennis. He went to prep school. He was a high achiever—smart and competitive. But as a teenager, he felt the tug of the wilderness. By sixteen, he realized he felt more at home in the woods than in the city, and he dropped out of school.

Grant began to learn from his uncle, who was a logger. He moved to Gold Bridge, a town north of Vancouver. Though he was where he wanted to be, he began to realize how logging hurt the environment. He saw machines clear-cutting the land—taking down all the trees in an area. Loggers scraped away the soil down to the rock underneath. Grant thought that nothing would be able to grow there again.

Well suited to outdoor life, Grant learned to do more than lumberjacking. At various times, he also worked as a gold miner, a rock driller, and a blaster. In the 1970s, he earned a forest technician's degree, and he proved to be adept at it. His job was to figure out where to build roads through the wilderness so large trucks could gain access to more trees. He was a tireless worker. He ran his own lumber company for a while.

Logging is one of the most dangerous jobs on land. Loggers can be hit by falling trees, maimed by chain saws, and stabbed by sharp cuts of wood. Sometimes these workers are victims of accidents that require an arm or a leg to be amputated. Some are even killed on the job.

Grant had almost a superhuman tolerance for tough conditions. One of his neighbors observed that Grant could do the work of three "normal" men. When two grizzly bears chased Grant one day, he saved himself by scrambling out of range of where they couldn't smell him. Once he shipwrecked a kayak on an island near Alaska and survived alone for twelve days before being rescued. One winter, when the air temperature was thirty-five degrees below zero, he took a dip in the Yukon River—and stayed in the frigid water for fifteen minutes. When he emerged, the water on his body froze and icicles dangled from his hair, but he felt fine.

In 1978, Grant married a nurse named Margaret, and they had three children. Grant built his family's house, which was two-and-a-half stories tall with a wonderful view of the forest. Margaret called Grant "indestructible." However, their marriage was not indestructible, and they separated in 1991.

Though Grant had made a living in the logging industry, he had felt conflicted about it since he was a teenager. On one hand, those jobs had allowed him to work in the environment he loved best. On the other hand, those jobs required him to damage that same environment. By the early 1990s, he was mailing letters to voice his disapproval of certain logging practices to judges, the press, the government, and even the Queen of England. He also sent letters or field reports to lumber company executives— including people he worked for or wanted to work for.

Loggers were cutting down trees for profit at a rapid pace. In these letters, Grant passionately and intelligently urged officials to leave more of the forest standing. He was worried that, before long, there might not be any trees left. Some people thought he was out of step with the times. But he was actually *ahead* of his time, because protecting the environment would soon become a more common cause.

Though Grant had a valid point, he sometimes went to extremes to express it. He had begun to hear voices when no one was around. Most likely he had begun to suffer from mental illness, possibly schizophrenia, which ran in his family.

Then Grant got an idea that he thought would deliver his message even more clearly.

Canada's largest lumber company was MacMillan Bloedel (later bought by a company called Weyerhaeuser). In the 1960s, MacMillan Bloedel had agreed to protect the area of the forest surrounding the golden spruce because it was so important to the Haida. The company didn't allow any trees on that section of land to be cut down.

Healthy trees are usually green, so Grant believed the golden spruce was a sick tree. He was angry that the lumber company cut down masses of healthy trees in the forest around it but left this one unhealthy tree standing.

So Grant decided he would cut it down himself.

— — — —

On the rainy night of January 20, 1997, the temperature was just above freezing on Graham Island. The previous night, Grant had stayed at the Golden Spruce Motel. Now he stood across the Yakoun River from the golden spruce itself. He held inflated garbage bags that contained a small chain saw and other equipment.

After swimming across the sixty-foot-wide river, he gazed up at the golden spruce. It is not known what kind of light source Grant brought, but he must have had something or it would have been too dark to see. The golden spruce was bright in daytime, but it didn't *literally* glow.

He fired up the saw.

Because the location was remote and the outdoor conditions were unfavorable, no one would have been near enough to hear the buzz of the saw. The trunk of the golden spruce was almost a foot wider than Grant's height. Even for an expert woodsman like Grant, it probably took several hours to cut into it as deeply as he did.

But he did not cut all the way through the trunk. He left a narrow band of wood to hold up the tree. He knew the next significant gust of wind would finish the job for him.

He swam back across the river and took a ferry back to Prince Rupert, a port town on the British Columbian mainland. He gave the saw to a man he knew. The man did not know what Grant had just done with it. When the man found out, he got rid of the saw immediately.

The day after attacking the golden spruce, Grant faxed a letter admitting it to MacMillan Bloedel, Haida leaders, Greenpeace (an organization that protects the environment), local newspapers, and the police. He wrote: "I didn't enjoy butchering this magnificent old plant, but you apparently need a ... wake-up call." Grant questioned if it made sense for people to condemn him for injuring just one tree to make a point when loggers were cutting down many trees all the time to make a profit. He told a reporter that the people around him should "see a person who is normally very respectful of life and has done a very disrespectful thing and ask why."

The police arrested Grant for criminal mischief and the illegal cutting of timber. The tree was valued at more than five thousand dollars. Grant was ordered to stand trial the following month.

Two days after Grant chainsawed the golden spruce, it toppled to the bank of the river. Sitka spruces can live eight hundred years, so the golden spruce had not yet reached middle age.

The community was devastated. The Haida were deeply sad and angry. They wanted revenge, as did other locals. Some people wanted to kill Grant. The tree was a loss for culture, science, and tourism. Native Americans, environmentalists, and even loggers—groups that did not always agree—now had something to agree on: This was an outrage.

Many saw Grant as an ecological terrorist. Grant seemed to see himself as an environmental hero. At least one Haida appeared to agree. He supported Grant's action because he felt that the logging company had arrogantly made a decision (to protect the golden spruce) that was not even theirs to make.

The Haida asked that the tree be left where it fell, alongside its stump. Many Haida felt guilty because they had failed to keep the tree safe. Some also feared that their people might soon be gone—the old legend about the golden spruce said that they would admire the tree until their last generation. Now that the tree was dead, did that mean *they* were the last generation? The Haida held a memorial service for the golden spruce, which they called an "ancestor," as if it were a human relative. The service was open to the public. This tree that started as a teardrop-shaped seed ended with a torrent of actual teardrops.

Grant spoke on the phone with Guujaaw, a Haida leader. "He didn't seem crazy," Guujaaw said afterward. "He sounded normal . . . as if what he'd done was no more than throwing a rock through a window." When Guujaaw told Grant the Haida origin story of the golden spruce, Grant quietly said, "I didn't know that."

He didn't say if he would have still cut down the golden spruce if he *had* known that it had symbolic meaning for the Haida. But now he did sound a bit remorseful.

Grant's court date on Graham Island was set for February 18, 1997. He did not want to fly or take the ferry to Graham Island. He thought that people might attack him on the way. Instead, he decided to kayak across Hecate Strait, the body of water that separated the British Columbia mainland from the Queen Charlotte Islands. Hecate Strait was sixty miles across and could have rough currents. And it was winter.

Before leaving Prince Rupert, Grant bought three hundred dollars' worth of food and camping gear, including a stove and an ax, as if he was planning a longer trip. He called Margaret to tell her he was leaving. She called the police, who tried to talk Grant out of attempting the crossing. He was not breaking the law, but the police had a responsibility to stop a person from putting himself in danger. That day, however, the police let Grant go. Perhaps they believed that if anyone could make it across, it would be Grant Hadwin.

Close to dusk on February 11, as a storm moved in, Grant set off. The wind was fierce and the waves were formidable—up to ten feet high. Grant did not make it to Graham Island that night—but he did survive.

In the morning, he returned to Prince Rupert for warmer clothes. The next day, he paddled off again. On February 14, someone saw Grant in the water twenty-five miles north of Prince Rupert.

That may have been the last time anyone saw him alive.

Margaret was not immediately worried. She knew Grant could handle the wilderness. But Grant's daughter's birthday was March 1, and Grant didn't call. *Then* Margaret began to worry.

Police in Canada and Alaska investigated. They were receiving at least one report a week of a Grant sighting, but none led to his discovery. People exchanged guesses about what could have happened to Grant. He might have been hit by a boat or been shot by someone angry at what he had done. He could have drowned. He could have landed on any of the many islands in the area and retreated into the wild. He had often talked of wanting to move to Siberia, in Russia, so perhaps he finally did.

In June 1997, a marine biologist came across Grant's kayak and some of his other belongings on a beach of uninhabited Mary Island, which is part of Alaska. Mary Island is seventy miles northwest of Prince Rupert and five miles from any other land.

To the biologist, it looked as though the wreck had happened within the past month. The kayak was banged up but still intact. The camping gear was in excellent condition. Investigators could not tell for sure if Grant had landed with the equipment, but one fact was especially curious. The ax found on the beach was above the high-tide mark. It was too heavy to float, which means that someone would have had to carry it ashore.

Grant loved his children. The fact that he has not contacted them may be the strongest indication that he is dead.

Years before Grant destroyed the golden spruce, scientists had taken a few branches from it to see if they could grow another tree like it at the University of British Columbia. After the golden spruce fell, more cuttings were taken. The Haida planted one cutting in a park and enclosed it in a fence with barbed wire at the top. Another cutting was planted next to the stump of the original.

No one knows if the golden spruce—or Grant—will ever return. One way they may live on is in the culture of the Haida. Both the tree and the man were real. But as the Haida tell future generations the story of what the man did to the tree—ending with the man's unsolved disappearance—the story may become legend.

PLAY THAT SONG AGAIN
MUSICIAN HENRY GRIMES

In the mid-1960s, jazz musician Henry Grimes was everywhere.

Many other musicians—including some of the most renowned of the day—hired Henry to play on their albums or during their live performances. Henry had what they called a big sound—some said the biggest sound in the business.

It wasn't technology that made Henry a musical giant—in those days, musicians didn't use electronic amplifiers. It wasn't his giant instrument, the double bass—the one that resembles an oversized violin and which musicians hold in front of them as they play standing up.

What gave Henry Grimes a big sound came from inside Henry Grimes. He was born with musical talent and with the drive to succeed in a competitive industry.

This made it all the more surprising when, in 1969, Henry

abruptly disappeared from the music scene—and, it seemed, from the planet. The man who had been everywhere was suddenly nowhere to be found.

— — — —

When Henry Grimes was born in 1935, it was almost as if he was joining an orchestra rather than a family. His father played trumpet. His mother played piano. His twin brother played clarinet and saxophone. Their older sister loved to listen to music. His parents worked in a type of café called an automat, but Henry thought both of them had spent time as professional musicians before he was born. However, he never heard them play in their home in Philadelphia.

By age twelve, Henry was a fan of a type of jazz music called swing. In junior high school, he took up classical violin. In high school, he learned to play the tuba, the English horn, and percussion. It was almost as if he was becoming an orchestra all by himself.

His artistic talent didn't end with music. He also wrote and drew his own comic strip, which he then distributed to classmates. They eagerly awaited each weekly installment. He wasn't the most talkative student, but he wasn't exactly shy, either.

Henry played violin in the school orchestra. He also jammed with jazz groups after school. A fellow musician who was in one of these groups admitted that they didn't sound very good.

The high school Henry attended focused on music. It was there, around age fourteen, that he discovered the instrument that would become his favorite, the double bass. He took to it immediately and word spread. The all-city orchestra had asked Henry to join.

From 1952 to 1954, Henry was a student at the prestigious Juilliard School of Music in New York City. Each school day, he traveled to New York from Philadelphia. Juilliard allowed him to study bass with a member of the New York Philharmonic and play bass in the opera orchestra. He was also playing jazz with musicians in clubs and other establishments.

The cost of (and commute to) Juilliard became too much for Henry, so he had to drop out. However, he was beginning to get regular jobs playing with other musicians, some of whom were big names in jazz, such as the singer Anita O'Day. Henry moved to New York, where many of the gigs were. He also began to travel around the United States and to Europe to perform live. Some of this music was also broadcast on the radio.

In 1957 and 1958, Henry was a member of a quartet organized by accomplished saxophonist Gerry Mulligan. The group performed live and also recorded music. At the same time he began working with Sonny Rollins, another saxophonist and jazz great. Sonny, who was not known for complimenting others often, called Henry a "fearless musician."

In 1958, Henry appeared at the popular Newport Jazz Festival in Rhode Island—playing in five different groups. A few of the groups included some of the most beloved musicians working at that time, including big band leader Benny Goodman and jazz pianist Thelonious Monk. Even when Henry was playing with people who were already famous, more and more people began to notice *his* rhythm.

Henry was able to work with musicians of many genres and styles. Some who played stringed instruments like Henry used a technique called *arco*, which means they ran the bow across the strings. Others preferred *pizzicato*, which means they plucked the strings with their fingers. Henry could do both extremely well. (At times, his fingers had calluses a half-inch thick from pizzicato.)

Whichever method musicians practiced, they loved working with Henry. He had not only a big sound but a big heart, too.

He became respected and trusted. When Charles Mingus, a well-known double-bass musician, wanted to perform with one other double-bass musician, he chose Henry.

The 1960s was an especially experimental time for music. Henry was a leading force in free jazz—a type of jazz played without a planned harmony or melody. Musicians playing free jazz essentially make up a song together as they go. With free jazz, they are free to play what they feel, not notes printed on a page. Henry's free jazz sound was a change from his earlier style.

He continued to perform and record with an impressive list of musicians. By the middle of the 1960s, he had played on fifty record albums. For most of them, he was a sideman—a musician hired as a part of a group. In 1965, he recorded *The Call*, his first album as a bandleader—meaning he was the star. Bandleaders generally earned more money and had more job security.

However, after *The Call*, Henry did not record another album as a bandleader. Artistically, he was doing well—he had plenty of fans. He had proven his talent onstage and in the recording studio. Yet financially, he was struggling. He knew he didn't promote himself as much as he probably should, and sometimes he didn't get paid as much as he was promised.

In 1968, Henry was offered work in San Francisco. He did not know how soon he would get more bookings in New York, so he decided to go. He and a drummer named Clarence Becton made a road trip out of it, driving across the country from New York. Henry's double bass (which he had named Brunhilda) was too big to fit inside the car, so he strapped it to the roof. As they drove through desert regions, the sun's heat cracked the bass.

In San Francisco, Henry's dog, Chica, went missing, deeply saddening Henry. And with his bass damaged, Henry was on the verge of losing something else dear to him.

After completing the musical work that brought him to San Francisco, Henry tried to find more opportunities there. When he couldn't, he relocated again, this time to Los Angeles. He landed a few gigs, but it was becoming increasingly difficult to play Brunhilda, so he brought the bass to a repair shop. A repairman said it would cost five hundred dollars to fix, but Henry couldn't afford that—so he sold the repairman his beloved bass for the same amount. He believed this loss was only temporary. He believed he would be able to come back for it (or get another) before too long.

But then like Chica, like Brunhilda, like the last note of a sad song, Henry lingered for a moment . . . then vanished.

— — — —

Years passed, and Henry's family, friends, and fellow musicians heard nothing from him. A book about jazz published in 1977 and reprinted in 1999 stated that "it is generally believed that Henry Grimes died in California in the 1970s." According to a 1986 jazz magazine, Henry had died in late 1984.

Also in 1986, teenager Marshall Marrotte went into a music store. He liked punk rock, but the music the store was playing grabbed him. He asked who the artist was, and an employee told him "Henry Grimes."

As Marshall grew up, jazz—and Henry—stayed with him. As an adult, Marshall became a social worker in Georgia. As part of his job, he helped homeless people try to locate their relatives. That meant he often had to search through official documents such as birth and death certificates, medical records, and court papers.

He had heard that Henry had disappeared. Rumors tended to be about Henry's death, but some claimed that he was still alive. Among the rumors: He had dyed his hair green and become an actor; he was a minister; he was homeless. Marshall decided to see what more he could find out. On nights and weekends, over several years, he applied the detective skills he'd picked up from his job to try to track down what happened to Henry.

In the fall of 2002, he learned that a man named Henry Grimes was living in Los Angeles in a single-room-occupancy hotel, a rental unit in which people with little money can get a private room. The building was in a poor neighborhood, and it was dirty and dangerous. Fights often broke out in the halls or outside, and the police would come.

Marshall called the hotel. Because it didn't have phones in the rooms, someone was sent to get the Henry Grimes who was living there. As Marshall waited, he heard people shouting or arguing. Even through the phone, it sounded like a rough place. The seconds seemed to be moving in slow motion. Marshall could not wait to find out if he had found *his* Henry Grimes.

He had indeed.

After all those years, the person who rediscovered Henry was not a relative, an old friend, or a former colleague, but a stranger.

The following weekend, Marshall flew to see Henry. He found a man in a tiny room who was poor but in good health and fairly good spirits.

The sixty-six-year-old musician began to tell the thirty-year-old social worker what he had been doing since 1969.

Toward the end of the 1960s, the hustle of the New York music scene had been wearing Henry out. (He also didn't like the cold weather.) He planned only to leave the city—not music itself. But after he sold his double bass, he realized that his emotions were not helping him create music. Instead, they were blocking him. He also was suffering from depression. After taking medication for it, he felt better. But he still didn't return to music.

Early during his missing period, he lived on the streets and in homeless shelters in California. During those hard times, his teeth fell out. For the past twenty years, he had lived in the same small room at the hotel.

To earn money, Henry had taken an assortment of jobs. He spent time as a janitor at a bowling alley and a custodian at a school. When doing cleaning jobs, he sometimes had to work the night shift. He even tried acting, meaning at least one rumor about him was true. At various times, he was a construction worker. He liked construction jobs because they kept him in shape. He would work, come home, fall asleep soon after, and repeat the routine the next day. It was an exhausting schedule, but it meant a regular paycheck—something he hadn't been able to count on as a musician. He also received Social Security money, but did not receive any royalty money for the music he had recorded.

Since he'd disappeared, he had not worked in music or even played privately. He didn't own an instrument. He couldn't afford one. He also hadn't gone to a jazz show and hadn't listened to any of his own recordings, though he did listen to other types of music on the radio, including gospel and rock. Yet he hadn't even seen a compact disc! Because he hadn't followed what was going on in the jazz world, he didn't know musicians were still playing free jazz, the style he helped form.

Though he wasn't playing or creating music, he hadn't stopped *thinking* about music. Technically, he *was* creating music, but "only in my head, and always in my head." He just didn't have the motivation to take the next step and actually try to play again. He said he was "waiting for something to happen." When that time came, he knew he could do it again.

In the meantime, he was creating something else—and putting it down on paper: poetry. He liked expressing himself with words just as he had with music and described writing poems as a type of musical expression. His output was steady, and his handwritten poems filled multiple notebooks. Another way he found peace was by practicing yoga.

Henry had been out of touch with his former life for more than three decades. He'd lost his address book and then lost touch with his family. No one was able to notify Henry when his father died. At times, Henry assumed that other musicians wanted to contact him but did not know how. At other times, he believed he would be forgotten. Henry was surprised to learn which of his friends had died since his disappearance. He didn't know *he* had been reported dead—twice.

Marshall played Henry some of his music. Henry said it was amazing he heard things in his own work that he hadn't realized before. It put him in a good mood, not a sad one. He said he had no regrets about not playing for decades. Music was a part of him whether he played or not.

Finally, Marshall asked the question Henry surely knew was coming: Did he want to play again? Henry admitted he felt some nervousness, but not because he doubted his ability. He wondered how people would respond to his music. "I didn't think that I was liked that much," he said modestly.

Marshall announced to the jazz world that Henry Grimes was alive and ready to make music again. The response was heartwarming—and, for Henry, overwhelming. Henry's hotel could barely keep up with the flood of phone calls it was receiving for Henry. Old friends and strangers mailed him CDs so he could get reacquainted with jazz. A few musicians told him that they thought they had recognized him on the street in Los Angeles, and one tried to approach him, but lost him in the crowd.

A jazz writer and publisher named Margaret Davis wanted to help Henry rejoin the jazz community. But first, Henry needed a bass.

Margaret contacted at least fifty musicians Henry had known, plus other musicians Henry never met—but who knew of him. She asked if anyone could help get a bass for him. Some said they wished they could, but couldn't. Some weren't nice about it. Some didn't respond at all.

When Henry disappeared, William Parker was seventeen years old. By the time Henry was rediscovered, William had become a famed bassist—one who had been influenced by Henry's music. William e-mailed Margaret that he would like to send Henry a bass.

On December 16, 2002, a delivery arrived at Henry's Los Angeles hotel—a big delivery. The crate was as big as a person and looked like a coffin. Henry unpacked it to find the bass William had sent. It came with the name Olive Oil—and it was green.

Henry had a bass again. (Soon he also had teeth again—in the form of dentures.)

He was deeply moved—and ready to move. He put the muscles he developed from construction work to good use: He carried the heavy instrument up three flights of stairs. Now he was ready to groove.

Margaret set up a fund at a New York string-instrument repair shop so that Henry could order any supplies he needed for his bass—for no charge. Meanwhile, in Los Angeles, Henry was practicing—constantly. For two months, he got to know jazz again with Olive Oil. The sounds coming from his room were not the kinds of sounds other people staying at the hotel were used to hearing there. "I didn't forget," Henry said about his music. "I couldn't forget."

Students at a nearby school heard of Henry and convinced the administrators to pay Henry to teach them music. He was blown away when a person who had been born after Henry disappeared knew of his work. Henry began to give private lessons. He also started to play in clubs again.

For too long, Henry had been alone. Now he was at the center of a circle of people including Marshall, Margaret, William, and the students, all working to get him back where he belonged. Henry had never felt so supported.

In 2003, Henry moved back to New York. The city felt different to him from when he last lived there decades earlier, perhaps more fast-paced or stressful. Yet once he started playing music, he relaxed and all felt right.

His return New York performance was at the Vision Festival— thirty-five years after he last performed in the city. The announcer said they were about to hear from a "very special guest." When the audience saw it was Henry, they gave him a standing ovation— before he started playing. He played as dazzlingly as he had when he was forty years younger. The event was covered in the esteemed *New York Times*. Other publications said Henry's revival was the greatest jazz story of the year, if not the decade. Later in 2003, he made his first music recording since the 1960s.

All About Jazz—New York, which calls itself the world's largest jazz music website, named Henry the "Musician of the Year" in 2003. It was one of numerous honors he has been awarded since his comeback. Perhaps the most moving honor was that musicians old and new wanted to play alongside him.

After Henry's return, he played in hundreds of concerts

and festivals in America, Canada, and close to two dozen other countries worldwide. He began to play the violin again and made his public debut as a violinist at age seventy. The following year, he published his first book, a collection of poems. He also got married . . . to Margaret.

"It sounds like a comedy, like I've come back from outer space," Henry said. "But I didn't have a chance to be surprised. I had to go to work and make the most of what's been offered to me."

Henry Grimes was playing again. And this time, he wasn't planning on going anywhere.

I LEAVE NO TRACE
NATURE LOVER EVERETT RUESS

Everett Ruess didn't mind being hungry. He wasn't bothered being chilly, or sick, or alone. As long as he could be in the desert, he could handle most anything—up to a point.

When Everett was sixteen years old, he made his first solo trek into nature, exploring various parts of the California wilderness. Over the next four years, he spent nearly all but the winter months hiking through more rough, sparsely populated terrain in California as well as Arizona, New Mexico, Utah, and Colorado.

Everett traveled without companions. (To be precise, he traveled without *human* companions. For some of his adventures, he had two burros, Pegasus and Pericles, and for a while, a white dog named Curly.) But he was never lonely. He kept up a brisk correspondence with his parents, his brother, and friends, writing and receiving letters at outposts throughout his journeys. His letters documented his love of the beauty and peace of the outdoors.

In November 1934, when he was twenty, he departed from a

small town in Utah, heading south to Arizona for the winter.

Winter arrived but Everett did not.

No one heard from him after that.

— — — —

Though Everett's *solo* travels began when he was a teenager, his overall travels began when he was just a baby. Between his 1914 birth and 1926, his family lived in five states: California, Massachusetts, New York, New Jersey, and Indiana. If Everett wasn't born with a wandering spirit, it was not long after when he developed one!

His father, Christopher, held numerous and diverse jobs, including a minister, a probation officer, and a sales manager. He had to move frequently for work. His mother, Stella, was a talented artist and poet. She taught art for a while and published a small booklet for her family of articles and poems written *by* her family—herself, Christopher, and their sons, Waldo and Everett. Everett's parents wanted him to share his creative side. His mother in particular had a deep creative influence on him.

When Everett was twelve and living in Indiana, he took an art class on Saturdays—in Chicago, more than an hour away. His artistic interests included clay modeling and wood carving. He wrote personal essays and poetry in high school and took more art classes on the side. He won an award for a poem he wrote. He loved reading adventure tales, including *1,001 Nights* (featuring a traveling hero named Sinbad the Sailor) and *20,000 Leagues Under the Sea* (featuring Captain Nemo, a man more at home in his submarine than in the crowded world on land).

In the summer of 1930, Everett set off on his first attempt to live off the land alone. For two months, he backpacked through parts of California, including the coast and Yosemite National Park. He slept alongside the ocean and under large pines. Though these were places he had not been before, he felt as though he had come home.

As part of Everett's artistic growth, he sought out successful artists for inspiration. During his California trip, he knocked on the door of a man who did not know him, a nationally known photographer named Edward Weston. Edward was impressed enough with Everett's pluck that he invited the young man to stay with his family for a while, and Everett did. Edward praised Everett's art, which encouraged Everett.

Upon graduating high school in January 1931, at sixteen, he wasted no time in escaping Los Angeles and returning to nature.

A Navajo Indian sold him a burro to carry his belongings, and Everett then spent almost the entire rest of the year trailblazing through Arizona and Utah. His parents were supportive. His father felt the experience would be as valuable for Everett as any course in school. When they could, his parents sent him checks for five or ten dollars.

On that trip, Everett visited the Grand Canyon and a Navajo reservation. At times he would walk uninvited into a Navajo lodge called a hogan—without knowing who lived there. This was so bold that some Navajos wondered if he was a witch. Yet Everett tended to gain the trust of Native Americans he encountered. He learned the Navajo language. A Navajo medicine man let Everett chant with him beside the bed of a sick girl. The Hopis painted him and let him join them in a traditional dance—the only non-native person so honored that year.

Everett's quest took him to some of the most remote, uninhabited locations in the United States. In some of those dusty places, he was the first recorded nonnative person to pass through. He came upon cliff dwellings no one else had seen for decades, perhaps longer. In a letter he sent home, he wrote, "I have seen almost more beauty than I can bear."

His days were filled with walking across shifting sand and among jagged rock formations, writing in journals and letters about what he saw, reading, painting, and pondering what mattered most to him in life. At night, he went over maps and read adventure stories by campfire light. He also read books of letters written by classical composers, which sometimes inspired him to sing opera to his burros.

Arizona called him again in the spring and summer of 1932, and Colorado, too. That fall, he enrolled at the University of California, Los Angeles. He completed one semester, but left in February 1933, desperate to get back to where he felt he truly belonged. He wrote to a friend, "I'm glad I went [to college], but I'm glad it's over."

Everett always set out alone, but he was not a loner. In a journal entry, he wrote that he enjoyed exploring on his own, but admitted that there were times when he would have welcomed a friend to appreciate it with. In addition to the famous artists and Native Americans he sometimes approached, Everett encountered cowboys, archeologists, hobos, and tourists. In fact, he sold and traded his woodcut (sometimes called woodblock) artwork to tourists, enabling him to extend his trips. Everett sent letters not only to his family but also to some of the people he had met on his journeys.

At various times, Everett called himself by other names. He may have been trying to prevent anyone from finding out more about him or contacting his relatives. One fake name he used was Lan Rameau. Two months later he became Evert Rulan. Then he went back to his actual name.

Small mishaps sometimes interrupted Everett's tranquil expeditions, but none stopped him from continuing. By experiencing accidents, Everett learned how to survive difficult and sometimes dangerous situations. Once, he disturbed a beehive, and bees swarmed him. He managed to yank off his shirt and pants and jump into a nearby stream. That drove off the bees, but then he saw that in addition to bee stings, he also had poison oak blisters all over his body.

Once, a wild bull charged him, but Everett was able to get away without injury. Another time he stepped on four rattlesnakes. Once, a horse he was traveling with fell into a river—drenching Everett's food, camera, artwork, and blank paper. One day, an unseen rodent chewed through a sack of his rice. Storms, extreme heat, and scorpions were just some of the other desert obstacles he had to be prepared for.

On top of that, Everett could be a daredevil. He rode broncos. He climbed nearly vertical cliffs using footholds that sometimes crumbled under his touch. "I personally was scared to death just watching him," said an archeologist who observed Everett sketching a waterfall from the edge of a four-hundred-foot cliff—during a rainstorm. Once, Everett reported going seventy hours without sleep. He took chances he could have avoided.

He bought food in towns along the way. In his journals he noted eating watermelon, peanut butter sandwiches, fried cheese sandwiches, bacon, trout fried in cornmeal, and pineapple. At times, however, he would go hungry for days—and he was fine with that. Once, two men were driving along an unpaved road in Arizona and saw Everett, who was sunburned and weak. They asked Everett if he would like a drink but Everett misunderstood. Though he was low on water, he offered *them* a sip from one of his two canteens.

A type of art he grew especially fond of—and good at— was woodcut printing. He would carve a landscape scene into a block of linoleum, press it in ink, and press the wet block on a piece of paper. That left a black-and-white image that was both simple and powerful.

In 1933, in California, Everett met several more successful artists. Ansel Adams was an accomplished photographer who became best-known for his black-and-white photographs of the landscapes of the American West. He and Everett traded prints. Everett also befriended painter Maynard Dixon and his wife, photographer Dorothea Lange, who took haunting photos of people during the Great Depression. Maynard showed Everett how to figure out what details one needs in—and what can be left out of—a piece of art. Everett called it the best art lesson he ever had, and probably considered it a life lesson as well.

A year earlier, Everett had been in college at UCLA. In September 1933, he was still in California, but in the great outdoors, not on a campus. He noted that other people his age were back in school that month. "But this is not vacation for me," he wrote. "This is my life." He told his parents that he wanted to keep going until he reached "the end of the horizon."

Everett's letters were always full of passion, such as when he wrote to Waldo, "I have been free of watches and clocks. I never wonder what time it is, because for myself it is always time to live." At times, however, he sounded depressed. Some of his comments—both written and spoken to people he met—revealed that he felt he might not come back from the wild. In 1933, he wrote to Waldo, "I don't belong in the world." He seemed to love life, but did not seem to think he would have a *long* life.

One passage in another 1933 letter to Waldo was especially alarming: "I'll never stop wandering. And when the time comes to die, I'll find the wildest, loneliest, most desolate spot there is." A letter that came after this described how he moved on from any campsite he had used: "When I go, I leave no trace."

In March 1934, Everett went home and saw his parents and brother. When he left about a month later, his family didn't know it would be the last time they would see him.

Throughout 1934, Everett continued to journey around the Southwest, including the red rock canyons of Arizona and Utah. In a September letter to Waldo, he wrote, "In my wanderings this year, I have taken more chances and had more and wilder adventures than ever before. And what magnificent country I have seen—wild, tremendous wasteland stretches, lost mesas, blue mountains rearing upward from the vermilion sands of the desert . . ." In yet another letter, he wrote, "I have been flirting pretty heavily with death, the old clown."

Though Everett's words were scary, Everett's family could do little to try to help him or find out exactly what he meant. Their only option was to respond with another letter. Everett was deep in the wilderness and could not easily be reached any other way.

In the fall of 1934, Everett arrived in Escalante, Utah. The town was so isolated that it did not receive many strangers, especially that time of year. Everett's clothes were ragged from the harsh desert conditions. He camped on the edge of town. During his short stay, he enjoyed activities that he couldn't when in the wild—he saw a movie and went to a dance. He told children stories and let them ride his burros. Nice as it may have been, he didn't want to settle in Escalante any more than any other town. He feared that if he met a woman and fell in love, he would have to give up his time in nature, and he didn't want to do that.

After selling some of his prints, *he* sent his *parents* ten dollars with a note reminding them that he said he'd give them money when he made his first million. He seemed to think he was on his way.

On November 11, 1934, Everett sent his brother what would be the final letter. He painted his scene in words: eating roasted meat and potatoes by the fire and hearing the gentle jingling of the bells around his burros' necks. He also wrote that he preferred "the saddle to the streetcar and star-sprinkled sky to a roof." He told his family that he was in a spot so remote that he likely would not be able to get a letter to them for at least two months.

A week after he left Escalante, he camped with two sheepherders. Then, somewhere near the Colorado River, Everett Ruess vanished into the wilderness he had predicted would take him.

Perhaps he had finally reached the end of the horizon.

His family never heard from him again.

— — — —

Two months passed and, true to his word, Everett had not contacted his parents. When a third month came and went with no word, they ached with worry. A letter they sent him was returned as "undeliverable."

Volunteers searched the canyons for him. They tried to signal him by lighting fires and by firing guns. Native American trackers searched water holes hoping to find a sign that he had taken a drink there.

In March 1935, a search party found Everett's two burros in Davis Gulch, a barren, steep-walled canyon. The animals were in a man-made pen with a good supply of creek water to drink and plant life to eat. Whoever built the pen clearly had cared for the animals.

The searchers also found burro equipment and candy wrappers in the area, but no belongings of Everett's—and no trace of Everett himself, except for a few footprints that led to nothing.

They did come across one other curiosity. "NEMO, 1934" was carved into the stone wall of a cliff dwelling near the pen. The same was scratched above the door of an abandoned Native American dwelling a mile away. Given Everett's love of the character Captain Nemo from *20,000 Leagues Under the Sea*, it seems likely that Everett was responsible for the markings. "Nemo" means "no one" in Latin, so Everett may have been describing how he felt unimportant when compared to the majesty of nature. The Nemo graffiti may have been signs of where Everett had been, but shed no light on where he had last gone.

People continued to search intently for half a year. In June 1935, Everett's parents came to search themselves, but they, too, found nothing. They came also to see the places their son had seen and meet the kind people who had helped look for him. Everett's friends offered to help his parents if they could. Some who had received letters from Everett forwarded them to his parents in case they contained clues that could help solve the mystery.

In July 1935, Everett's parents received a letter from a

California miner named Neil Johnson, in which he wrote that based on what three Navajos told him, he believed Everett was alive. Johnson and John Terrell, a reporter for the *Salt Lake Tribune*, tried to hire a Native American guide to help them search. Some native people they asked were afraid to take the job. If Everett was dead, they might find his spirit, and the spirit might not be happy about that.

An experienced Native American tracker named Dougeye agreed to lead Neil and John on a search—if they did not take a camera. That modern piece of technology made Dougeye uncomfortable. After scouring the area for two days, Dougeye concluded that Everett wasn't buried in Davis Gulch or else he would have found the grave. Dougeye believed that Everett had gone deeper into the canyons and had not come out.

Over the years, various Everett sightings were reported. One man claimed Everett served on a ship with him during World War II. Multiple people said that Everett married a Navajo woman, had a child, and lived on a reservation. Other sightings came from Utah, Mexico, and even as far away as Florida. However, none of the sightings was confirmed to be Everett.

In 1940, Everett's father wrote to *Desert Magazine*: "Whether

Everett is alive or dead, he is at peace now. He left us and the world in twenty years with more to remember and to treasure than could be required of an average hundred years."

More potential clues surfaced every so often. In 1957, at an abandoned campsite in Arizona, scientists found what seemed to be Everett's canteen, and razor blades from the Owl Drug Company—the brand that Everett used. In 1983, someone noticed another "Nemo" scratching on a canyon wall. In 1999, a mound that some felt may have been Everett's grave was dug up—but underneath was only more dirt. Authorities have examined skeletons found in the desert to see if any were a match for Everett.

Everett was officially declared dead in 1963. Some people imagined that he died by falling off a cliff or into a crevice, drowning, or some other accident. Others—including his family—thought he was murdered either by a Native American who disliked outsiders or by cattle rustlers who thought he was a government agent sent to stop them. At least one man confessed to killing Everett, but he did not seem believable and authorities found no evidence supporting his confession. Some believed Everett committed suicide, but his family and friends responded that he loved life too much.

Then there are those who thought he just withdrew fully from civilization. In other words, they think Everett *didn't* die, or at least not in 1934.

We all have dreams. We don't all have the courage to follow them—but Everett did. That is why ballads have been written about him and why Waldo felt his brother touched so many. Everett left behind at least 175,000 pages of writing and numerous art prints. The Southern Utah Wilderness Alliance uses one of his pieces of art as its logo. If he had survived, his work may not have generated the interest it has.

Everett became one of those Western figures whose real life seems like a legend. For more than seventy years after he vanished, people hunted for the truth about what happened to him. They told his story on camping trips. Navajo medicine men had visions of him. The pen in which his burros had been discovered in 1935 was still standing as of 2009. And it was that same year in which the mystery of Everett Ruess's disappearance may finally have been solved—by a man who didn't know the name Everett Ruess.

In the 1930s, a Navajo man named Aneth Nez had witnessed three members of the Ute tribe murder a young white man. The killers left with the white man's burros and Aneth buried the stranger's body. Aneth was afraid to mention the incident to anyone—until 1971, when he told his granddaughter Daisy Johnson. Then came another long wait. Daisy passed on the story to her brother, Denny Bellson—but not until 2008. Denny wanted to try to find out if the murder his grandfather saw really happened.

Using the information his sister shared, Denny was (directly or indirectly) responsible for a series of remarkable discoveries. First he located the desert burial site, about sixty miles from Escalante. Next he contacted the FBI to investigate, after which a Navajo archeologist was granted permission to remove the remains there for examination. Additional scientists determined that the bones were from a white male between the ages of 19 and 22—a description of Everett Ruess in 1934. Professors compared the skull fragments to 1933 photos of Everett and found them to be an almost-certain match. Finally, scientists compared the DNA of the bones with the DNA of Everett's closest living relatives, four nephews and nieces. Given the similarities between the DNA, the scientists concluded that Everett may have been found.

However, shortly after the announcement, other experts raised doubts. After examining photographs of the remains, both the state archeologist and the physical anthropologist of Utah speculated that the remains may rather have come from an American Indian. The teeth were shaped in a way common among American Indians and relatively uncommon among Caucasians. Also, the skeleton showed no evidence of dental work in two teeth in which Everett had fillings. These observations prompted the Ruess family to request more testing.

If the remains do prove to be Everett, his family intended to cremate them and release them over the Pacific Ocean. In life, Everett was a wandering spirit, and his family's decision will, in a sense, allow him—even in death—to keep on wandering, only on water instead of land.

Some of the territory Everett explored remains as desolate and untouched today as it was in the 1930s. Yet it no longer hides the final secret of a man who thought it was a place so beautiful that neither words nor art could fully express it.

VERY HARDER THAN I THOUGHT
KINDERGARTNER HANNAH KLAMECKI

Dave Klamecki and Hannah Klamecki were best friends. Dave was sixty-two years old. Hannah was five years old. They had the same last name because Hannah was Dave's granddaughter.

Living forty-five miles south of Chicago in the small town of Momence, Illinois, they enjoyed spending leisure time on the Kankakee River, which passed through town. Mike Klamecki—Dave's son and Hannah's father—called the pair "river rats."

As a young man, Dave was in the army and served in the Vietnam War. Afterward, for more than thirty years, he worked in a steel mill in Chicago. In 2000, Mike and his wife, Carol, had their first child, Sam—but the baby died a day after birth. The family was devastated. When Carol and Mike had Hannah two years later, Dave changed. Some might say he melted with joy.

He realized that life is too short to *wait* to do what you love, so he retired early. Living by the river had been a dream of his, so he moved with his wife to a cottage in Momence, just a few miles from Mike and Carol and only a few paces from the Kankakee. He wanted to spend more time with his family, and with Hannah.

On Wednesday, June 13, 2007, Dave and Hannah went out on the river. They didn't return by dinnertime. They had still not returned by nightfall. The family knew that Dave knew how to handle himself on the water, but still, they worried.

They could not yet know that there would be both a sad and a happy ending to Dave and Hannah's disappearance.

— — — —

Right after finishing kindergarten, Hannah got a special treat. She went to visit her grandparents for a whole week—alone. Her two younger sisters, three-year-old Rachael and two-year-old Chloe, were staying home with their parents.

Hannah's grandfather Dave was a fisherman. A sign in his cottage read FISHING STORIES TOLD HERE. June 13 was a hot day—which was not a surprise in Illinois the week before summer officially began. Dave loaded his sixteen-foot aluminum fishing boat with supplies, including life jackets, bathing suits, and a pail. He planned to take Hannah out for an afternoon swim in the river, which he did often himself.

For Dave, the river was not only a place to catch bass and cool off. It was a source of beauty. To protect it, he was a member of an organization that regularly cleaned out trash that people had carelessly dumped there.

As they spent time together outdoors, Dave taught Hannah to respect nature—don't litter, for example. He also showed her what he knew about surviving in nature. Hannah's father hadn't been interested in fishing as a boy. Finally Dave had a young person to share that passion with.

Dave loved that river, and now Hannah did, too.

The two steered toward one of their favorite spots, a small beach on Whirlpool Point, an island in the river a mile and a half from where they set off. It was safe to land the boat there, play on the beach, and swim nearby. However, a bit farther out, the depth of the water increased from a few inches to eighteen feet.

The island was also close to Whirlpool Bend, a point where two tributaries rushed into the river and created strong currents. Whirlpool Bend was considered the most dangerous part of the river. Dave was a strong swimmer and had never had trouble before.

The last time someone saw Dave and Hannah together was at seven that evening.

At ten-thirty, the family called the Momence Fire Department. Four hours later, they found Dave's boat on Whirlpool Point. Hannah's life jacket was in it. Her footprints were sprinkled over the sand around it.

But neither Hannah nor Dave was anywhere in sight.

— — — —

Soon the search for Dave and Hannah grew bigger. The state police, the Illinois Department of Conservation, and the local sheriff's river patrol joined the rescue effort.

A helicopter swept over the river and the acres of woods along the riverbank. A team of divers searched underwater. The searchers also used sonar, a system in which a device sends out sound waves that bounce back if they "bump into" an object underwater. These "bounced back" waves then tell the device where the underwater object is.

Meanwhile, the Klamecki family was trying to cope with their loss—which they hoped was only temporary. Mike and Carol spent Thursday crying and waiting and trying to explain to their other two young daughters what was happening. To Carol, "every breath out was a prayer; every breath in was a prayer." Hannah's younger sister Rachael went to the river and called out to Hannah.

She asked her to come home because it was "time to eat."

Because Mike had heard that Hannah's life jacket was still in the boat, he found it harder to keep the faith. Hannah had started taking swimming lessons in the past year, but she was hardly ready to swim alone in a river. The river was fast and the surrounding woods were vast, home to animals, including deer and coyotes. If lost in those woods, even an adult would have a tough time finding his way out.

Mike was a church pastor. His congregation supported the family in asking for God's help in returning Dave and Hannah safely. On Thursday night, the church held a prayer vigil and a hundred people attended. Twenty-four hours had passed since Dave and Hannah had vanished, but to the family, the day had felt endless. They were thankful that so many professionals were searching for their loved ones, but they themselves felt powerless—except for their prayers.

At dark, the searchers stopped using sonar. However, the search continued—and the family prayed—into the night.

At eight Friday morning, the searchers made a tragic discovery. They located Dave's body in the water, near the island where he'd left his boat. He had drowned. The Klameckis were heartbroken.

In grieving for Dave, they couldn't help but also think of Hannah. "If my dad couldn't make it," Mike said, "there was no way she could make it, because he was like Joe River, Joe Fisherman, Joe Outdoorsman, and she's just five years old." She was afraid of bugs, the dark, getting dirty, and strange noises.

Dave was a fisherman until the end. Mike took comfort knowing that his father had died doing what he loved, *with* someone he loved. "Not many people can say that," Mike said.

The family prayed yet again, asking God to bring Hannah back that day.

Though Mike knew the search team was doing a thorough job, his feeling of helplessness grew too much to bear. He decided he was going into the woods to search for Hannah himself.

But before he could, and thirty minutes after the family learned about Dave, the phone rang again. What they would hear might be terrible, but they had to answer.

This time, it was good news. The searchers had found Hannah—rather, *she* had found *them*.

— — — —

Just before 10:30 AM, Hannah had walked out of the woods. She was three-quarters of a mile from where the search team thought she would have come ashore.

"Who's that little girl?" one searcher asked as Hannah approached. "That can't be her, can it?"

Hannah told them her name. Kankakee Sheriff's Chief Deputy Ken McCabe said, "That's a tough little girl."

The search team offered Hannah water and a banana. She asked for a chocolate cookie.

Fire Chief Dave Horn radioed a message: "She's alive! She's alive!"

She was tired, dehydrated, and barefoot. Scratches covered her body, with a few bug bites and a bit of poison ivy rash mixed in. She had splinters and thorns in her bruised feet. Her fingernails were choked with dirt. Yet overall, McCabe said, she was in "pretty good shape."

She was also carrying mulberries, saving them so her grandmother could use them to make a pancake breakfast.

When the Klameckis were told that Hannah was sitting in an ambulance eating a banana, the house erupted with screams of relief. There were hugs all around and more tears—continued tears of sadness over Dave and new tears of happiness over Hannah. Mike said, "It was like every single prayer that had been uttered aloud for her was answered."

Even Chief Deputy McCabe, who'd been with the police department for eleven years, cried.

During his twenty-nine years with the fire department, Fire Chief Horn had never seen a situation like Hannah's. "All I can say, it's a miracle."

Another officer saw *two* miracles—that she survived the water and that she survived the woods, especially for as long as she did. She made it through two nights—nearly forty hours—alone in a hot, scary environment. In that forest, she could have wandered in the wrong direction so easily, yet she didn't.

Hannah's family believed she pulled through because of two factors: God's blessings and Dave's teachings.

They rushed to her. She was wearing a T-shirt and bundled in blankets. She munched on her banana and watched her family jump—literally—for joy around her. Carol said that the period Hannah was missing was "the longest days of my life."

The ambulance took Hannah to the hospital. The emergency-room doctors found her to be fine, aside from minor scratches and cuts. She enjoyed a grilled-cheese sandwich and french fries. Squeezing a new teddy bear, she took a much-deserved nap in the hospital. Her parents sat by her side.

After she woke, she was released from the hospital. The family arrived at the cottage close to dinnertime. Hannah and her two sisters were reunited in a flurry of kisses and squeezes.

At first, Hannah didn't say much. As her shock wore off, she was able to answer questions about what had happened. Since she was young and the experience had been traumatic, everyone understood that she might not remember some details or might remember them differently than they really happened. In any event, a sad yet astounding story began to take shape.

Hannah had been playing on the beach of the small island where Dave had brought his boat ashore. He went into the water. Hannah, wearing inflated floats on her arms, followed him in. As they swam, Hannah felt her grandfather push her without warning. The push was strong enough that her head dipped underwater for a moment.

When she surfaced, she didn't see her grandfather.

He had pushed her toward the bank of the river. When she was close enough, she grabbed a branch and pulled herself ashore. She still didn't see her grandfather.

The adults hearing this had a hunch that they knew what it meant. They would never be able to find out for sure, but they believed that Dave had saved Hannah's life. It sounded like he had been pulled under by a current, so he pushed her away from it and toward safety. His last act was not for himself but for his granddaughter.

"I was stuck in a little forest," Hannah said. It scared her like "a haunted house." She lay under a tree and tried to sleep, but the chirping of the bugs was too loud. She also felt cold. "And when it was night, I tried to look for my grandma and grandpa's cottage. I went searching all over the world to look for the cottage. But it was very harder than I thought."

The next day, she kept searching. She tried to follow the river but got lost—she said she saw a large house and went over a bridge. She didn't drink or eat all day.

"I don't know how she did it," her father said later. "I couldn't have done that."

While her family was praying for her, she was praying right back. "Please help me find the cottage. And help me find my grandma and grandpa."

Her bathing suit was itchy, and it had gotten muddy, so she took it off. She somehow endured a second night in the woods. She found the searchers the next morning.

Her parents were proud. Through the ordeal, their daughter—who liked to dress up like a princess—showed that she was no damsel in distress. She was her own knight in shining armor.

Hannah wanted to know where her grandfather was.

"I told Hannah part of the reason she's safe is because Grandpa knew what to do and knew to push her in the right direction," Mike said. "She said she was sad. We told her it was okay to cry. I hugged her and held her, and we talked about good things, baiting hooks, fishing on the boat."

Hannah asked why she lived and he didn't. Her father said that her grandfather was a hero and she nodded.

— — — —

The Klameckis had to mourn and celebrate at the same time. On Saturday, they invited friends for a barbecue—Dave had loved to grill. Hannah's friends were eager to show her how glad they were that she was okay. They wanted to give her hugs and toys.

On Monday, Hannah quarreled with her sister. On Tuesday, she quarreled with her parents. They were happy about that. It meant she was becoming herself again. Her feet still ached, however, and she wanted to be carried sometimes.

Wednesday was Dave's funeral. Hannah drew a picture for

her grandfather—it showed the two of them on the river. So many people came to pay their respects that they couldn't all fit in the chapel. During the service, Hannah sometimes fidgeted and sometimes sat still. The family had displayed photos of Dave around the chapel—Dave dressed as Santa, Dave holding up a fish he caught. Many of the photos also included Hannah—Dave changing her diaper, feeding the ducks with her, roasting hot dogs with her. The last slide of a slide show created to honor Dave showed a single word: "hero."

After the funeral, the mourners went outside. Because Dave was a veteran, the Momence Honor Guard gave him a twenty-one-gun salute. A military officer presented Hannah's grandmother with an American flag. Hannah tried to climb a tree, but an adult stopped her.

Perhaps it was just her way of trying to say good-bye to her outdoorsman grandpa.

In church the following Sunday, the community gave Hannah a Certificate of Bravery.

Later that month, Hannah got to do something that ended up being an honor for both her and her grandfather. In front of a stadium of people, she threw out the first pitch at a Chicago White

Sox baseball game. She waved to the crowd, and they cheered her like she'd just hit a home run in the bottom of the ninth—only louder.

"I feel a little nervous, but my mom and dad was standing by me," Hannah said. Perhaps she had felt the same way during her time in the woods.

And perhaps the spirit of her grandfather, who was a lifelong Sox fan, was part of that cheering crowd.

He was *certainly* standing by Hannah in the woods.

PILOT, POET, AND PRINCE
AVIATOR/AUTHOR
ANTOINE DE SAINT-EXUPÉRY

Antoine de Saint-Exupéry was about to crash his plane . . . again.

Africa's Sahara Desert was coming up fast. Pilot Saint-Exupéry (Saint-Ex to his friends) and his navigator, André Prévot, braced themselves to hit the ground. With a muffled bang, sand walls sprayed up around the plane. Both men managed to walk away from the accident relatively unhurt. They did not know where in the desert they were, and they had no way to call for help.

As a pilot, Saint-Ex's bravery—and evidently his luck—were greater than his skill. Fellow pilots may have felt that crashing was as much a part of his flying experience as landing. He was also a writer, and he found himself (yet again) caught in a real-life adventure that would make a great book.

This time, the impact was only the start of the ordeal. Saint-

Ex had survived the crash, but now he and André had to survive the desert. Specifically, they had to survive heat, lack of water and food, isolation, and potential capture (or worse) by hostile tribespeople.

Yet he and André did overcome it all, enduring four days before being rescued. Saint-Ex would go on to crash more planes. The last of those crashes would end not in a rescue but in a mystery that continued for more than fifty years.

— — — —

Perhaps Saint-Ex took to the open skies as an adult because he was always stuck in the middle as a child. He was born the third of five children in Lyon, France, in 1900. Before he turned four, his father had a stroke and died. Aside from that tragedy, his childhood, overall, was a happy one.

Saint-Ex and his siblings lived with their mother in a castle in eastern France. Creativity flowed through their days. The kids painted, put on plays, and frolicked in the long hallways of the castle or the spacious park around it. Their mother was their primary artistic influence, playing piano for them and fostering a love of books and stories.

Before Antoine's nickname was "Saint-Ex," it was "King

Sun"—"king" because he acted as a ruler of their castle playground and "sun" because of his blond hair. However, he was not a king—or even a prince—in the classroom.

When Saint-Ex was nine, the family moved from the countryside castle to the city of Le Mans in northwestern France. He attended religious and boarding schools in France and Switzerland—all good institutions—but he was not a good student. Sometimes his appearance was sloppy—his sunny locks not combed neatly, his necktie not hanging straight. He did not pay attention and would get into trouble.

Yet at sixteen, he discovered that he liked to write—first poetry, later short stories. A friend who saw past Saint-Ex's unremarkable academic performance and recognized his talent said, "One day he will be famous."

Writing was not the only activity Saint-Ex discovered in his youth that would become a passion of his adult life. He failed his final exam for university preparatory school and failed the entrance exam to the naval academy. After studying but not especially liking architecture for two years, he joined the military in April 1921. That would finally allow him to do something he truly loved—flying.

He began pilot training, but that was not the first time he had flown in an airplane. Air travel was still in its infancy in 1921, but back in 1912, it was so new that most people had never seen a plane in person, let alone been a passenger in one. That summer, the Saint-Exupéry family had vacationed at the castle where they used to live. Saint-Ex would sneak off to an airfield within biking distance and watch planes take off and land. He befriended the people who worked there. One pilot was so impressed with the twelve-year-old boy's enthusiasm that he took him up for a ride—in a homemade plane.

Saint-Ex was so taken by the experience that he wrote a poem about it later that same day. He also "converted" his bike into a plane by attaching "wings" made of a bedsheet. "You shall see when I take off on my plane," Saint-Ex said in his most booming voice. "The crowd will shout: 'Hurrah, Antoine de Saint-Exupéry!'"

To Saint-Ex's disappointment, the military had less majestic plans in mind for him in 1921. He was assigned to a ground position—no flying. Determined as always, he took private flight lessons. Though the lessons were expensive, they paid off—he earned his civil pilot's license. This led to the military supporting him in pursuing his military pilot's license.

On July 9, 1921, Saint-Ex made his first solo flight. After completing his pilot training the next year, he happily transferred to the French air force. In a 1923 letter to his mother, he wrote, "I adore this occupation. You cannot imagine the calmness and solitude one finds at 4,000 meters [13,123 feet] of altitude, alone with the engine."

Soon, however, Saint-Ex was forced back to earth. He got engaged to Louise de Vilmorin. After one of Saint-Ex's flying accidents in which he broke several bones, Louise's family said they did not want her to marry a man whose job regularly put him at such risk. In 1923, Saint-Ex agreed to seek out "safer" work in Paris.

Over the next three years, he hopped from one job to another—tile factory supervisor, bookkeeper, car salesman. He was not good at some of them, and he didn't like any of them. In between, he wrote stories, but he was still miserable. He felt stuck again, this time not between siblings but between walls, and he wanted out—and up.

Saint-Ex and Louise decided to call off the wedding. In 1926, he eagerly returned to flying. He also sold a short story to a literary magazine—his first published work. Fittingly, the story was called "L'Aviateur"—"The Aviator." It was about a pilot who gets depressed whenever he is not in his airplane.

For Saint-Ex, things were indeed beginning to look up.

— — — —

Saint-Ex could be sociable, but he was usually on the shy side. A fellow pilot once said Saint-Ex "behaved like a little boy who was telling secrets." Like the character in "The Aviator," Saint-Ex was most at home alone in the air.

The flying job he'd begun in 1926 was quite a departure from his work in the military. For starters, he had to learn how things had changed in civil aviation since he last flew. He worked for a commercial airline company called Aéropostale flying mail from Europe to Africa. The company required him to first take a course in plane repair, in case he went down and was the only person available to fix it. His first route took him from Toulouse, France, over Spain, then over the Sahara Desert, and finally down to Senegal, a country on the west coast of Africa.

The work was dangerous both in the air and on the ground. Planes were still rather primitive, equipped with few controls or safety features. Some Aéropostale planes were rickety open-cockpit biplanes from World War I, still in use though the war had ended in 1918. Sandstorms could be fierce, as could tribespeople, who sometimes would shoot at planes overhead. Yet none of this was enough to deter Saint-Ex.

In 1927, he was named director of a remote airfield in the Saharan portion of the country of Morocco, an area controlled by Spain. The conditions were rough. Dangerous rebels roamed the area. Saint-Ex lived in a wooden shack with bars on the windows and a barbed wire fence around it. Sand was on one side, sea on the other—so close that waves would smack the outer wall of the shack. He slept on a thin mattress made of straw. His desk was a board placed between two barrels. On the desk sat a typewriter on which he was writing a novel. He also had clothes and a wash basin, but little else. And he loved it.

Saint-Ex had several responsibilities at the airfield. Mail planes landed there every eight days. He assisted them by refilling their gas tanks and helping with any repairs. Otherwise, he was often alone.

He prevented boredom by making friends with locals, Spaniards and Arabs alike. Sometimes they even helped Saint-Ex with another of his responsibilities: pilot rescue. If a plane crashed in the desert, he would rush out to search for the pilot and the wreckage. A search party including locals was more efficient than a single searcher. Either way, it was scary work. "Looking for two airplanes lost in the desert, I covered 8,000 kilometers [4,971 miles] in two days," Saint-Ex said. "More than three hundred men pursued me, shooting at me as if I were a rabbit." He received an award for courage on the job.

Two big changes affected Saint-Ex in 1929. First, his first novel—the one he was writing in the shack—was published. *Southern Mail* was inspired by the mail route he had flown from France to North Africa. The book describes how the pilots flew as fast as they could, despite increased risk to themselves, to prove to postal customers that air mail was superior to mail transport by railroad or steamship.

Second, he left the Sahara for another dangerous job in another difficult environment—directing a company in Argentina that flew mail over the Andes Mountains. In 1930, he met a woman named Consuelo. He took her flying that same day and within hours said that they would get married one day. The next year, they did.

Also in 1931, Saint-Ex's second novel, *Night Flight*, came out. Based on his time in South America, the book revolves around a young pilot named Fabien. At the end of the story, Fabien and his plane vanish, never to be found.

When the company in South America shut down in 1934, Saint-Ex returned to France. He did some writing as a magazine journalist, traveling to cover stories in Spain, Germany, and Russia. He was a test pilot for airlines, including Air France, but made too many mistakes to keep at it.

In 1935, Saint-Ex and a navigator, André Prévot, set out to break a record and win a prize. If they could fly from Paris to Saigon, Vietnam, faster than anyone had before, they'd receive 150,000 francs. On December 30, close to twenty hours after they took off, their plane went down in the Libyan Sahara Desert. Saint-Ex may have been good at crashing, but he was also good at surviving.

Both he and André survived the crash itself, but their chances of further survival were grim. In one account, Saint-Ex said they had only a thermos of coffee, chocolate, and a few crackers. In another, he remembered their supplies as some grapes, two oranges, and a bit of wine. Either way, it wasn't much. They managed to drink dew that formed on the wings of their battered plane, but without more water, they would dehydrate quickly and die.

The days blurred together. Both men began to see and hear

things that weren't there. By the third day, their bodies no longer held enough water to sweat. Meanwhile, unknown to them, many people in France were praying that their beloved writer and his companion would somehow be okay.

On the fourth day in the desert, those prayers were answered. Saint-Ex and André crossed paths with a man on a camel who helped them to safety.

In 1937, Saint-Ex attempted another race, this one between New York and the southern tip of South America, and survived another crash, this time in Guatemala. His injuries were more serious than any he'd suffered in his previous accidents. He broke his skull, banged up his left shoulder, and fell into a coma for days.

Saint-Ex wrote about his grueling four days in the Sahara in a book called *Wind, Sand and Stars*. It came out in 1939 and won major awards. The same year, World War II broke out.

Though he still felt pain from his various crashes, Saint-Ex wanted to serve his country. His weakened physical condition was not his only obstacle to rejoining the military. He was also nearly forty years old, past the age when soldiers typically participate in combat. But Saint-Ex would not take no for an answer. After repeatedly trying to convince military officers to let him fly, they finally approved his request to rejoin the French air force. Part of Saint-Ex's responsibility was to fly over enemy territory to gather information. Sometimes pilots with that task had to fly low, which made them easier targets.

In 1940, France surrendered to Germany, but Saint-Ex wasn't ready to give up the fight. He decided to move to America. While he felt guilty leaving his homeland in hard times, he believed he could help convince the United States to enter the war by telling firsthand stories about the invasion of France (even though he didn't speak English). His publisher helped him get out of France. His ship arrived in America on the last day of 1940. Though he expected to stay only a few weeks, that plan didn't pan out.

The U.S. War Department allowed him to stay in the country if he did occasional work for them such as reviewing photographs taken from planes to identify regions of foreign countries. Saint-Ex found the work annoying. Adding to his frustration, Saint-Ex was too old to be a pilot for America once the country entered the war after the Japanese attack on Pearl Harbor in December 1941. Being far from France already troubled him, and now he couldn't fly, either.

Saint-Ex and Consuelo moved into an apartment in New York City and also rented a big house on Long Island. Their city apartment was a penthouse. Saint-Ex described it as "almost like being up in a plane."

— — — —

Saint-Ex did not feel at home in America. He heard little from family and friends in France because almost no one besides his publisher knew that the celebrated author had gone to New York (the secrecy was at the request of the War Department). However, he did find joy at times, such as when he saw his books for sale in Bloomingdale's department store.

He and Consuelo did not have children of their own, but Saint-Ex enjoyed playing with the children of visiting friends. They would launch paper airplanes or hurl water balloons out of his top-floor windows. He even threw scraps of paper off the Empire State Building to watch them fly. At times, Saint-Ex could come across like a child himself.

From summer to October of 1942, Saint-Ex didn't only act like a child—he also wrote about one. The result was *The Little Prince*.

On the surface, the book is a fairy tale about a little prince from a little planet who comes to Earth and meets a pilot whose plane has crashed in the desert. Its deeper meaning is about the meaning of life itself. It was inspired in part by his own desert crash of 1935. To some readers, it was a children's book. Others saw it as a book *about* a child but *for* adults. Either way, it was nothing like anything he'd published before.

Finding New York City too loud, Saint-Ex had written *The Little Prince* in Long Island. He illustrated it, too. In fact, it was the illustrations that led to the book. For years, Saint-Ex had been doodling a character on letters, restaurant tablecloths, and assorted other places. "I asked him who he was," Saint-Exupéry said. "I'm the Little Prince," the boy drawing told him. It is said that the wife of his publisher suggested that Saint-Ex build a book around the character. At a drugstore, he bought children's watercolor paints and brushes, which he'd never used before, and got to work.

First thing in the morning, Saint-Ex began drawing and painting in the library of the house. As models, he referred to a doll for the Little Prince, a poodle for a sheep, a boxer (the dog, not the fighter) for a tiger. When the sunlight moved into the parlor, he relocated there to write. When it came to research, he could be precise about details. Once, he asked a friend who worked at the *New York Times* if she could find out how many stars were in the sky.

He often worked late, drinking soda and coffee. He had a habit of waking guests in the middle of the night to read them what he'd just written or show them what he'd just drawn. At times he would rouse his wife to make him scrambled eggs.

In 1943, *The Little Prince* was published in America in both English and French. The same year, Saint-Ex left New York and returned to France. By then, America had entered the war, and Saint-Ex wanted to fight with the Americans in North Africa. He was, of course, even older than the last time he'd tried to rejoin the military, but he again talked his way back into the French air force.

Saint-Ex was not well. His life of adventure had worn him down at a young age. He had high fevers regularly. Once, he fainted while flying. He continued to ache from the bones he had broken over the years, so much so that he could not get into a flight suit without help.

The type of plane he was assigned was new—and fast. To fly those particular planes, pilots were required to be no older than thirty-five. Saint-Ex was forty-three. He had not been properly trained. Sometimes he got confused or made mistakes, once causing thousands of dollars of damage. He was allowed to fly on the condition that he would not go on more than five missions. Of course, he charmed his way past that restriction, too.

For his eighth mission, he was asked to fly over the Rhone River in France to look for German troops and take photographs. He had recently sent a letter to his wife in which he wrote, "I am very, very far from you. I cannot tell you where I am. But I am so near you, who lives in my heart."

He took off under clear skies from Corsica, an island in the Mediterranean Sea, at 8:45 AM on July 31, 1944. His commanding officer expected him back by 12:30 PM. When Saint-Ex had not returned by 1:30, his squad worried. An hour later, there was still no sign of him, and they knew he would have run out of gas by then. An hour after that, the military officially declared Saint-Ex missing.

Eight months after that, even though no one knew for sure if Saint-Ex was dead, they held his funeral.

— — — —

Upon hearing of Saint-Ex's disappearance, Anne Morrow Lindbergh, wife of famed aviator Charles Lindbergh, said, "There is a terrible difference between lost and dead." Theories about Saint-Ex's fate swirled in the air like the bits of paper he'd sprinkled from the Empire State Building. A woman had reported witnessing a plane slam into the water on August 1; a male body in a French uniform was found shortly after, but it was in such bad condition that it could not be identified. Many people assumed Saint-Ex either had been shot down or had crashed due to yet another blunder. Some suspected he had been depressed and crashed on purpose.

For more than half a century, despite extensive searching, no known clues surfaced. Then in 1998, a fisherman off the coast of Marseille, France, pulled up something in his net besides fish—a silver bracelet tangled in seaweed, attached to a piece of what appeared to be a flight suit, and engraved with the names of Saint-Ex, Consuelo, and Saint-Ex's New York publisher. The Saint-Exupéry family said it was a fake and sent it to be analyzed, but did not announce any result. The fisherman stood by his story. Six years later, he returned to the site where he'd found the bracelet and laid a wreath on the water.

When a scuba diver heard about the bracelet, he recalled seeing plane debris in the vicinity some years earlier. In water between one hundred and three hundred feet deep, hundreds of parts were scattered under the sand of the seafloor, indicating that the plane had probably exploded on impact. By 2000, after studying records of planes that had crashed, the scuba diver believed that those parts were from Saint-Ex's plane. It took until 2003 for the French government to give permission to bring up the pieces. Once that happened, a serial number on a tail piece confirmed that the plane was indeed Saint-Ex's. The examiners didn't find bullet holes on any of the pieces. However, because only part of the plane was recovered, they could not say for sure that the plane had *not* been shot down.

The bracelet had been found one hundred and thirty miles from where Saint-Ex's flight path would have taken him. The plane wreck was only a mile from the spot where the bracelet was found. Both were fewer than fifty miles from where the unidentified body had been discovered back in 1944. Ocean currents could explain the distances.

Yet some fans did not want any of it to reveal what had happened to Saint-Ex. They preferred his fate to remain unknown. It makes for a better story. Some members of Saint-Ex's family also did not want to believe that the mystery was solved. They felt that these discoveries implied that Saint-Ex had strayed from his mission, which might lend more proof to the unpleasant theory that he had committed suicide.

In 2008, an eighty-five-year-old German man named Horst Rippert told a story that either solved or reopened the mystery, depending on whom you ask. Horst was a German pilot during World War II. He claimed that he had shot down the kind of plane that Saint-Ex was flying on July 31, 1944—and that he did it over the area where the wreckage had been found.

Horst recalled hearing about Saint-Ex's disappearance only days after July 31, 1944, and had an uneasy hunch at the time that he was responsible, but he did not say anything publicly until after the wreckage was discovered. He felt sad and guilty because he had read Saint-Ex's books as a young man. "I didn't see the pilot and, even so, it would have been impossible for me to know that it was Saint-Exupéry," he said. Flight logs that could have proven whether or not Horst's story is true were destroyed during the war.

The Little Prince had received mixed reviews when it was published in 1943. However, after Saint-Ex vanished, it went on to become not only his bestselling book but also one of the bestselling books of all time. *The Little Prince* has been translated into at least 230 languages and still sells millions of copies a year.

Tributes to Saint-Ex abound in France and beyond—in one

case, far beyond. In 2000, the airport in his hometown of Lyon was renamed in his honor. The chief gardener of Paris named a new breed of blue rose after him. Before France switched to the euro as its standard unit of currency in 2002, Saint-Ex's face was on the 50-franc note. A monument to him stands in Morocco near the airfield where he served as director in 1927.

Even a distant asteroid bears his name. As for whether a lonely Little Prince lives there, that may remain as much a mystery as what caused Saint-Ex's plane to plummet into the sea one warm wartime day.

ABOUT THE AUTHOR

Marc Tyler Nobleman is the author of more than seventy books including *Boys of Steel: The Creators of Superman*. He writes regularly for Nickelodeon and is also a cartoonist. At noblemania. blogspot.com, he reveals the behind-the-scenes stories of his books, from exciting research moments to risky promotional efforts.

When he was a baby, in August 1973, someone in his family vanished. His cousin Leonore, who had sometimes looked after him, went to a bus station, bought a ticket to somewhere, and never came back. Leonore's husband hired detectives to find her, but despite years of searching, none could. Her fate remains a mystery, except to her.